USDA United States
Department of
Agriculture

Forest
Service

North Central
Research Station

General
Technical Report
NC-264

A Revised Managers Handbook for Red Pine in the North Central Region

Compiled and Edited by:

Daniel W. Gilmore and Brian J. Palik

A Joint Publication of the

USDA Forest Service and University of Minnesota

Contents

**North Central
Research Station**
USDA Forest Service

1992 Folwell Avenue
Saint Paul,
Minnesota, 55108

Published 2005

www.ncrs.fs.fed.us

List of Contributors & Reviewers

John W. Benzie, USDA Forest Service, North Central Research Station (retired)

Charles R. Blinn, University of Minnesota

Thomas E. Burk, University of Minnesota

Thomas R. Crow, USDA Forest Service, Research and Development

Andrew J. David, University of Minnesota

Daniel W. Gilmore, University of Minnesota

Amy L. Harder, SAPPI, Cloquet, Minnesota

Howard M. Hoganson, University of Minnesota

Beth Jacqmain, Aitkin County Land Development, Aitkin, Minnesota

Brad Jones, Itasca County Land Department, Grand Rapids, Minnesota

Steven A. Katovich, USDA Forest Service, Northeastern Area State and Private Forestry

Allen L. Lundgren, USDA Forest Service, North Central Research Station (retired)

Timothy J. Mack, Consulting Forester, Hanover, Maine

Michael E. Ostry, USDA Forest Service, North Central Research Station

Brian J. Palik, USDA Forest Service, North Central Research Station

Eric K. Zenner, University of Minnesota

List of External Reviewers

Thomas J. Dean, Louisiana State University

Alan R. Ek, University of Minnesota

Alan Jones, Minnesota Department of Natural Resources

Michael A. Kilgore, University of Minnesota

Thomas McCann, USDA Forest Service, Superior National Forest

Linda M. Nagel, Michigan Technological University

H. Michael Rauscher, USDA Forest Service, Southeastern Research Station

Scott D. Roberts, Mississippi State University

Alan Saberniak, USDA Forest Service, Hiawatha National Forest

Ronald W. Severs, University of Minnesota

Gary Swanson, USDA Forest Service, Chippewa National Forest

Myra Theimer, USDA Forest Service, Superior National Forest

Gary Wyckoff, Plum Creek, Escanaba, Michigan

John C. Zasada, USDA Forest Service, North Central Research Station (retired)

Management Guides for Red Pine —
Their Evolution and Why We Need Them

Red pine (*Pinus resinosa* Ait.), also known as Norway pine has been the most widely planted species in the Lake States region of North America over the past 70 years. As a result, the red pine cover type in the Lake States has increased more than fivefold to almost 1.9 million acres. Because of its widespread occurrence and economic value, red pine has long received close attention from researchers and forest managers. In 1914, Theodore S. Woolsey, Jr., and Herman H. Chapman published a 42-page U.S. Department of Agriculture Bulletin entitled, "Norway Pine in the Lake States." This early management guide, based on careful observations and measurements by field foresters, served as the primary guide for managing red pine stands for more than 30 years.

During the latter two-thirds of the 20th century, employees of the USDA Forest Service, State governments, universities, the Canadian government, and others established long-term studies of red pine. As measurements and results from these studies became available, red pine guides were periodically revised and updated. Most of these guides focused on establishing and managing red pine stands to improve timber growth.

Since the late 1900s, however, the objectives of management, especially on public lands, have broadened beyond timber output. Land managers are now being challenged to address questions not answered by existing guides. Despite their widespread use, the red pine management guides produced to date have several deficiencies: 1) They focus on managing the stand as an isolated unit, without considering landscape concerns; 2) they focus almost exclusively on timber production, with little attention to recreation, aesthetics, wildlife, water, or other objectives; 3) they apply primarily to pure, single-aged red pine stands and have little to say about stands of mixed species or ages; 4) they are poorly linked to landscape ecology and to vegetation and soil types; and 5) they classify site productivity of red pine stands almost entirely with site index.

Because existing guides no longer meet the needs of contemporary land managers, we have developed this new handbook for managing red pine with multiple objectives in mind. As a multidisciplinary team of public and private foresters, researchers, and practitioners, we have attempted to eliminate some of the deficiencies noted above by bringing up-to-date information from many disciplines to bear on a wider range of red pine management issues.

About the Authors:

Daniel Gilmore is an Assistant Professor of Silviculture with the University of Minnesota, St. Paul, Minnesota.

Brian Palik is a Project Leader and Research Ecologist with the USDA Forest Service, North Central Research Station, Grand Rapids, Minnesota

Managing Stands in the Context of Ownership Goals

While silviculture is applied at the scale of forest stands, it is important to consider the implications of stand management within the context of varying ownership goals across the landscape. A useful approach for doing this is to look at the different goals of management, including production management, extensive management, and reserve management, and how and where these goals are applied. In principle, these are not discrete categories, but general treatment groups that overlap and grade into one another. For our purposes, intensity refers to the degree of disturbance associated with silvicultural treatments, and management goal is defined by the degree to which producing wood fiber is the driving objective.

Production management is often associated with high capital investments to ensure rapid dominance by desired species. This includes treatments such as thinning to maximize growth and pruning to improve the quality of wood. Fertilization, irrigation, site preparation, control of competition, and planting of genetically improved stock are tools used to achieve these ends. The establishment and tending of plantations is typically considered to be production management.

Extensive management is the broadest category among the three and has been the most common approach in North Central forests. Compared with production management, extensive management applies over larger areas and has lower impacts, lower costs, and lower return on capital investment. Even-aged management in natural forests falls within extensive management, as do individual tree and small group selection prescriptions. It may involve managing on extended rotations for old growth characteristics and timber, increased ecological complexity, and heterogeneity in forests that are also managed for wood. Important management goals, in addition to timber production, include enhancement of wildlife, water, recreation, biological diversity, and aesthetics.

The goals of reserve management include conserving and protecting natural areas from human-caused disturbances and may involve restoring the forest to some predetermined reference condition. In either case, financial return on investment or commodity goals do not apply. Reserve management can be intrusive or nonintrusive. When the goal is to restore a natural condition or process, treatments may be quite intrusive and intensive. Timber harvesting, logging or prescribed burning might be applied to retain early successional species, create desired structural features, reduce the threat of insect and disease outbreaks, control exotic species, or accelerate growth of large-diameter trees.

Many of the management guidelines for red pine that follow are framed around this principle of a gradient of management goals including: 1) production management, 2) extensive management, and 3) reserve management. The reader is reminded that the value of different management approaches is driven by landowner objectives. We do not advocate one approach over another, but simply present a range of options.

Ecological and Silvical Highlights of Red Pine

Before settlement, red pine made up an estimated one-third of the 22 million acres of pine forest in Minnesota, Wisconsin, and Michigan. The amount of red pine in the contemporary landscape—around one million acres—is greatly reduced from this total, due to uncontrolled timber harvesting, wild fire, and land conversion to agriculture and development. Today there is a greater proportion of aspen on the landscape.

On drier sites, red pine forests range from nearly pure stands to mixtures of jack pine, eastern white pine, aspen, paper birch, and oaks. On moister sites, red pine is found growing with eastern white pine, red maple, red oak, balsam fir, and white spruce. Red pine grows best on well-drained sandy to loamy sand soils, but is most common on sandy soils having site indices of 45 to 75 feet at 50 years of age.

Red pine is a shade-intolerant, long-lived species characteristic of drier sites and soils. Although individual trees can reach 400 years of age, most stands live no longer than 200 years. The species is best described as mid-successional. It often replaces early successional species such as jack pine and aspen, and in turn is replaced by eastern white pine and hardwoods.

Red pine is a fire-adapted species. Historically, natural stands with a significant red pine component were disturbed by frequent surface fires and less frequent crown fires. In combination, these disturbances helped perpetuate the species by controlling competing understory vegetation, preparing mineral seedbeds, and opening the canopy to promote seedling establishment.

Red pine flowers in the spring. Both male and female flowers are produced on the same tree. Cones ripen the following summer, dispersing seeds for up to a year. Good seed crops occur every 3 to 7 years. Timing seedbed preparation to good seed years is requisite for abundant natural regeneration of red pine.

Red pine has a variety of uses, including pulpwood, cabin logs, poles, and saw logs. Red pine forests, both pure and mixed, provide habitat for a variety of plant and animal species.

Red Pine Management Considerations

MANAGEMENT GOALS, OBJECTIVES, AND IMPLICATIONS

The following management action key (table 1) is based on the premise that stand-scale objectives fall largely within one or more of the three ownership goals: production management, extensive management, or reserve management. For each of these goals, the key guides the user through applicable decisions and refers him or her to sections in the guide that address details of particular actions. Where management objectives encompass more than one goal, for example, production management within multi-species stands, users can integrate information to address their specific needs.

To use the management action key, start with the first pair of numbered statements and choose the one that best describes your goal or situation. Follow this statement to a number, a recommendation, or a number and a recommendation. If a number is given, find the corresponding pair of statements and continue the process until you reach a final recommendation.

Table 1.—Management action keys for red pine management

Start	Condition or Goal	Go to or do
1.	Site is typical for red pine in the locale See Ecological and Silvical Highlights of Red Pine, p. 3	2.
1.	Site is not typical for red pine	4.
2.	Reserve management objectives dominate See Managing Stands in the Context of Ownership Goals, p. 2	*Go to Key A*
2.	Reserve management objectives do not dominate See Managing Stands in the Context of Ownership Goals, p. 2	3.
3.	Production management is the primary objective See Managing Stands in the Context of Ownership Goals, p. 2	*Go to Key B*
3.	Extensive management is the primary objective See Managing Stands in the Context of Ownership Goals, p. 2	*Go to Key C*
4.	Site is less productive (drier or wetter) than typical red pine site See Ecological and Silvical Highlights of Red Pine, p. 3	*Consider establishing or converting to site-appropriate species*
4.	Site is more productive than typical red pine site See Ecological and Silvical Highlights of Red Pine, p. 3; Site Quality Assessment, p. 9.	*Consider establishing or converting to site-appropriate species or intensive red pine production (Key B)*

(Table 1 continued on next page)

(Table 1 continued)

Start	Condition or Goal	Go to or do

Key A: Reserve Management

Start	Condition or Goal	Go to or do
1.	Red pine stand already established on site	2.
1.	No red pine stand currently on site	5.
	2. Stand is seedling size	3.
	2. Stand is not seedling size	7.
3.	Stand currently meets expectations for composition and structure Consider protection needs; see Damaging Agents, p. 29	*Reassess at later date*
3.	Restoration needs exist in terms of structure or composition See Managing Red Pine Stands for Ecological Complexity, p. 23	4.
	4. Stocking of red pine is unacceptably low	*5. Regenerate all or portions of site*
	4. Stocking of red pine is variable or stocking of other desirable species is inadequate or competition levels are undesirably high See Regenerating Red Pine, p. 13	*Fill plant and/or control competition; reassess at later date*
5.	No established stand on area	*6. Consider all regeneration options in light of Reserve Management goals*

5.	Established stand on area
	    Consider conversion and legacy retention prescriptions;
	    see Managing Red Pine Stands for Ecological Complexity, p. 23
		*6. Harvest in light of
		    Reserve Management goals*

	6. Good establishment conditions exist, free of undesirable competition
	    Consider regenerating multiple species;
	    see Regenerating Red Pine, p. 13 and Managing Red Pine
	    Stands for Ecological Complexity, p. 23
		*Plant or seed;
		reassess at later date*

	6. Inadequate establishment conditions exist
	    Consider regenerating multiple species;
	    see Regenerating Red Pine, p. 13 and Managing Red Pine
	    Stands for Ecological Complexity, p. 23
		*Prepare site; plant or seed;
		reassess at later date*

7.	Stand requires structural or compositional treatment in light of
	Reserve Management objectives
	    Consider variable density thinning, releasing co-occurring species;
	    underplanting additional species; see Stand Density, p. 19;
	    Managing Red Pine Stands for Ecological Complexity, p. 23;
	    consider protection and maintenance needs (e.g., prescribed
	    understory fire); see Damaging Agents, p. 29
		*Thin, release, or underplant;
		reassess at later date*

7.	Stand condition (structure and composition) meets expectations
	    Consider protection and maintenance needs (e.g., prescribed
	    understory fire); see Damaging Agents, p. 29
		Reassess at later date

(Table 1 continued on next page)

(Table 1 continued)

Start		Condition or Goal	Go to or do
Key B: Production Management			
1.		Red pine stand already established on site	2.
1.		No red pine stand currently on site	5.
	2.	Stand is seedling size	3.
	2.	Stand is not seedling size	9.
3.		Stocking and competition levels are acceptable for production management See Regenerating Red Pine, p. 13	*Reassess at later date*
3.		Stocking and or competition levels are unacceptable	4.
	4.	Stocking is unacceptable See Regenerating Red Pine, p. 13	8. *Replant*
	4.	Stocking is variable and/or competition levels are high See Regenerating Red Pine, p. 13	*Fill plant or control competition; reassess at later date*
5.		No merchantable stand on area	6.
5.		Merchantable stand on area See Regenerating Red Pine, p. 13.	8. *Harvest and consider all regeneration options in light of Production Management goals*
	6.	Will have merchantable stand in 20 years or less	7.
	6.	Will not have merchantable stand in 20 years	8.
7.		Consider waiting until merchantable size	*Reassess at later date*
7.		Prepare site now according to Production Management goals	8.
8.		Good establishment conditions exist, free of excessive slash and competition See Regenerating Red Pine, p. 13	*Plant; reassess at later date*
8.		Inadequate establishment conditions exist in the form of excessive slash, herbaceous or shrub competition See Regenerating Red Pine, p. 13	*Prepare site; plant; reassess at later date*
	9.	Stand is at rotation age for production management See Rotation Age, p. 22	*Harvest;* go to 8.
	9.	Stand is not at rotation age for production management	10.

10.		Stand requires thinning, crop trees require pruning, or competition control is needed
		    See Stand Density, p. 19; Pruning, p. 21;
		    Growth and Yield, p. 22; Damaging Agents, p. 29
			Thin, prune, or release; reassess at later date

10.		None of the above are required	*Reassess at later date*

(Table 1 continued on next page)

(Table 1 continued)

Start	Condition or Goal	Go to or do
Key C: Extensive Management		
1.	Red pine stand already established on site	2.
1.	No red pine stand currently on site	5.
2.	Stand is seedling size	3.
2.	Stand is not seedling size	9.
3.	Red pine stocking, competition levels, and species composition are acceptable for extensive management See Regenerating Red Pine, p. 13; Managing Red Pine Stands for Ecological Complexity, p. 23	*Reassess at later date*
3.	Red pine stocking, competition levels, or species composition are unacceptable for extensive management	4.
4.	Stocking of red pine is unacceptable See Regenerating Red Pine, p. 13	*8. Regenerate site*
4.	Stocking of red pine is variable or stocking of other desirable species is inadequate or competition levels are undesirably high See Regenerating Red Pine, p. 13	*Spot-plant red pine or other species; control competition; reassess at later date*
5.	No merchantable stand on area	6.
5.	Merchantable stand on area Consider restoration opportunities; consider legacy retention prescriptions; see Managing Red Pine Stands for Ecological Complexity, p. 23	*8. Harvest in light of Extensive Management goals*
6.	Will have merchantable stand in 20 years or less	7.
6.	Will not have merchantable stand in 20 years or less	8.
7.	Consider waiting until merchantable size before action to regenerate red pine	*Reassess at later date*
7.	Prepare site now according to Extensive Management goals; consider restoration opportunities and legacy retention prescriptions; see Managing Red Pine Stands for Ecological Complexity, p. 23	8.
8.	Good establishment conditions exist, free of undesirable competition Consider regenerating multiple species; see Regenerating Red Pine, p. 13; Managing Red Pine Stands for Ecological Complexity, p. 23	*Plant or seed; reassess at later date*
8.	Inadequate establishment conditions exist Consider regenerating multiple species; see Regenerating Red Pine, p. 13; Managing Red Pine Stands for Ecological Complexity, p. 23	*Prepare site; plant or seed; reassess at later date*

(Table 1 continued on next page)

(Table 1 continued)

Start	Condition or Goal	Go to or do

Key C: Extensive Management *(continued)*

Start	Condition or Goal	Go to or do
9.	Stand is at rotation age for extensive management objectives Consider legacy retention prescriptions; see Rotation Age, p. 22; Managing Red Pine Stands for Ecological Complexity, p. 23; Damaging Agents, p. 29	*Harvest, regenerate;* go to 8
9.	Stand is not at rotation age for extensive management	10.
10.	Consider standard or variable density thinning, pruning, release of co-occurring species, decadence creation, underplanting tolerant species; see Stand Density, p. 19; Pruning, p. 21; Managing Red Pine Stands for Ecological Complexity, p. 23.	*Thin, prune, release; reassess at later date*
10.	None of the above are required or desired	*Reassess at later date*

GENETIC CONSIDERATIONS IN RED PINE MANAGEMENT

Red pine is one of the most genetically uniform tree species. Nonetheless, small but significant differences among families have been detected for traits such as height and volume. Differences also exist among regions. For example, 11-year results from a replicated progeny test indicated that although good stands could be found in all regions, the seed sources from the Lower Peninsula of Michigan outperformed all other regions on eight of nine sites and ranked second on the ninth site (Wright *et al.* 1972). Also, differences in chloroplast DNA exist across the species' range suggesting that the postglacial history of red pine is more complex than originally thought (Walter and Epperson 2001). Collectively, this morphological and molecular data indicate that red pine has a complex evolutionary history and does possess genetic differentiation at the regional and family levels.

Production Management

In production management, the overriding goal is to optimize the return on investment from the growth and quality of wood products. As early as 1901, red pine was viewed as a potential plantation species. Historically interest has been focused on timber and fiber production. Despite this interest, few organizations have taken steps to produce improved red pine seed or specified improved red pine seedlings for their planting programs. Instead they have relied on seeds collected from native stands in the mistaken belief that improvements in growth were impossible or inconsequential.

Improved red pine seed can be provided through the establishment of seedling seed orchards, which are a relatively easy, cost-effective method for increasing the supply of genetically improved seed. Many of these orchards, established between the early 1960s and late 1980s, now produce operational levels of improved seed that are adapted to local growing conditions. Estimates of volume gain for these improved seedlings vary but the selection method used has an impact on the genetic diversity of the seed coming from these orchards (David *et al.* 2003).

Extensive Management

With extensive management, natural regeneration is the primary method of restocking the stand. Managers should take genetic considerations into account when choosing the leave trees that will produce seed for natural regeneration. Guidelines for selecting leave trees are based on research into heritability, which measures how much of a trait is controlled by genes as opposed to the environment. The higher the heritability the easier it is for field personnel to visually select trees with superior genes. In a native stand or population it is difficult to pick superior trees for traits such as height, diameter, or volume, because these traits have low heritability. It is much easier to identify trees with better than average genes for stem form, branch angle, and branch thickness, because these traits have medium to high levels of heritability. As a general rule leave trees should be disease free, and have straight stems with medium to thin branches that meet the trunk at a 90° angle. They should also be good self-pruners and have crowns balanced in height and width. Trees with large diameter branches and those with forked stems and irregular or misshapen crowns should be avoided.

Reserve Management

With reserve management, most trees will be retained, although some trees may be removed to facilitate restoration goals. Typically, selection for specific traits will not drive decisions about removal or retention. One caveat comes into play here: that of a minimum population size necessary to maintain a viable population. Although the pollination dynamics in small populations of forest trees is not well understood theoretical work has indicated that 50 breeding individuals are sufficient for maintaining existing genetic diversity in a population. In red pine the required number of breeding individuals is expected to be lower than 50 for two reasons. First, compared to other conifers red pine has lower levels of genetic variation, so fewer individuals would be required to maintain existing genetic diversity. Secondly, red pine can tolerate elevated levels of inbreeding with no loss of seed set or germination, (albeit with a loss of some height growth). Managers should bear in mind that the number of breeding individuals is not the same as the total number of individuals. Generally, the number of breeding individuals is lower because immature or suppressed trees may not produce pollen or cones, and other individuals may produce cones infrequently, or be asynchronous with the majority of the population.

ESTABLISHMENT CONSIDERATIONS

Site Quality Assessment

Managers and landowners often want to estimate potential growth before establishing a red pine stand. Understanding site quality and choosing a proper site can optimize tree growth and survival, and minimize the risk of insect and disease infestations. Site quality data can also help managers project growth and yield in established stands. This section provides a summary of existing site quality work and how it may be used to select sites for plantation establishment and identify sites for intensive management.

Several methods are currently used to assess site quality in the Lake States and Northeast, including site index curves, soil-site approaches, and vegetative and biophysical approaches. Depending on the size of their holdings, landowners may be limited in the range of site qualities available for red pine. In such instances, relative measures of site quality may be useful. For example, if landowners' goals include production, extensive, and reserve management, they may choose higher quality sites for timber production and lower quality sites where red pine occurs naturally for reserve management. On the other hand, they may wish to practice both timber management and reserve management on high-quality sites and extensive management on the remainder of their land holdings. In either case, an assessment of site quality would be important.

Site Index

Site index is the most commonly used method of assessing site quality in North America and is defined as the height of a tree at a base or index age, usually 50 years. Trees measured to determine site index should be over 30 years old and be in a dominant or codominant canopy position.

Site index curves for red pine that have withstood the test of time (Benzie 1977) are provided in figure 1. Carmean *et al.* (1989) conducted a review of site index curves for all species in North America in the 1980s. Seven additional site index curves for red pine are included in appendix A.

Figure 1.—
Red pine site index curves; based on the equation: height = site index $(1.956 - 2.1757$ $e^{-0.01644(age)})$ (Lundgren and Dolid 1970).

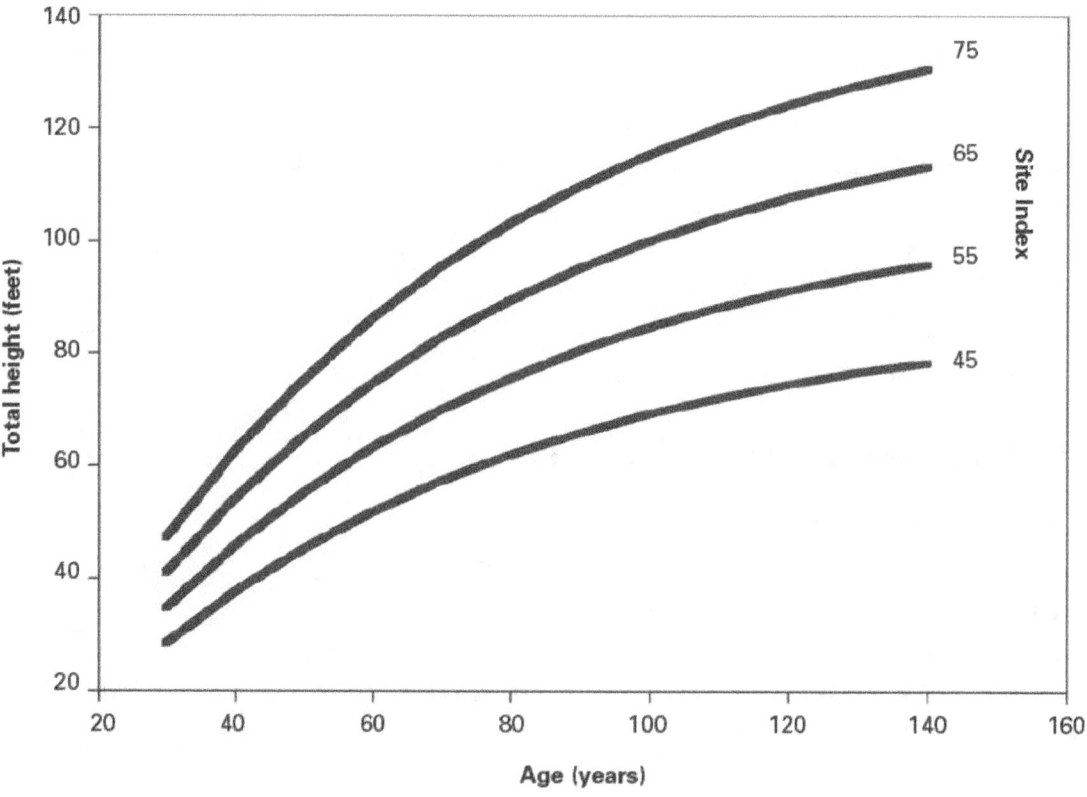

Growth Intercept

It is not always possible to determine site index directly. Records may not exist for a given stand before the establishment of a plantation, or the plantation may be considerably younger than the index age. Site index can be estimated in such cases by using the growth intercept method, which utilizes a designated period of early height growth as an indicator of site quality. To eliminate potential error associated with slow and erratic height growth, managers should measure internode length above breast height. The primary disadvantage of the growth intercept method is that early height growth patterns may not accurately reflect later height growth patterns. Tables 2 and 3 provide estimates of site quality for red pine based on annual internode growth above breast height.

Table 2.—Estimates of site index for red pine trees greater than 15 years old (based on the equation SI = 36.9 + 3.356GI − 192.474GI^{-2}, where, SI = site index and GI = length of 5 internodes above 8 feet). (Alban 1972a)

Length of 5 internodes above 8 feet	Site index
(feet)	(feet)
4	38
5	46
6	52
7	56
8	61
9	65
10	68
11	72
12	76

Table 3.—Site index estimates based on average annual height growth above breast height

Average annual height growth above bh	Site index
(inches)	(feet)
10	45
13	55
17	65
24	75

Red pine plantations are often established on sites occupied by other species. Or, a landowner may wish to convert another type of forest type to red pine. Site index for red pine can be estimated from other trees growing on such sites provided the site index for these trees can be determined (table 4).

Table 4.—Site index (in feet) conversions to red pine from jack pine, white pine, white spruce, and aspen site indices

Red pine	Jack pine	White pine	White spruce	Aspen
45	50	45	35	40
55	60	55	50	60
65	70	65	65	80
75	80	75	80	100

Soil-Site Approaches

Soil-site studies are undertaken to determine a relationship between site index and edaphic (soil-related) and other variables describing a particular site (e.g., aspect, elevation). Although soil-site studies typically have only regional applicability, they can be generalized across regions if studies from different regions have similar results. Results of eight soil-site studies (Hicock *et al.* 1931; Van Eck and Whiteside 1958; Wilde *et al.* 1965; Hannah 1971; Alban 1972b, 1974, 1976; Brown and Duncan 1990) across the range of red pine are summarized below.

Site index is positively related to improved soil drainage, a sandy loam soil texture, rooting depth, and thickness of the A and B soil horizons. Site index is also positively correlated with the presence of finer textured soil bands or layers totaling a thickness of at least 3 to 6 inches within 8 to 15 feet of the soil surface. Site index is negatively correlated to the percentage of gravel or rocks in the top 10 inches of soil (table 5). The percentage of soil organic matter, or soil carbon, has been found to affect site index both positively and negatively. Aspect and percent slope have relatively small impact on site index, although higher site indices tend to be associated with lower slope positions. Higher concentrations of soil N and P are also related to higher site indices.

Table 5.—Estimated site index for red pine plantations in the Lake States on well-drained sand to sandy loam soils[1]

Gravel or rocks in top 10 inches	Depth of A plus B horizons (inches)					
	5	10	20	30	40	50
Percent by weight	*Site Index (feet)*					
0	55	57	60	63	67	70
10	52	54	57	60	63	67
20	49	51	54	57	60	63
30	46	48	51	54	57	60
40	43	45	48	51	54	57
50	40	41	44	48	51	54

[1] Add 5 feet to site index on soils with bands or layers of finer textured material within 8 feet of the surface that improve water relations; subtract 5 feet from site index for natural stands (adapted for the Lake States from Alban (1976).

Other Considerations

It is important to consider that site index predicts the height of dominant or codominant trees in a stand at a given base age. Factors in addition to site index may be important in comparisons of productivity. For example, a side-by-side comparison of 40-year-old red pine and jack pine stands growing on the same soil showed that red pine had 55 percent more volume than jack pine. The red pine had produced 225 ft² per acre of basal area in 40 years, compared with 152 ft² per acre of basal area for jack pine. Red pine has an ability to grow at higher densities than other species.

REGENERATING RED PINE

This section provides an overview of site preparation, planting, and release treatments for red pine—practices that can help managers meet a wide range of objectives. Artificial regeneration is emphasized because relatively little work has been conducted on the natural regeneration of red pine and few managers have experience with the practice. Indeed, managers often favor direct seeding over plantation establishment. Limited information on red pine natural regeneration does suggest that: 1) natural regeneration is best on shaded mineral soil, 2) shading down to 25 percent of full light does not affect early survival or height growth, 3) mechanical site preparation has greater efficacy in reducing competing vegetation than prescribed burning, and 4) insects are a major cause of first-season mortality, especially in areas having higher amounts of light.

Site Preparation

Effective site preparation helps improve the growing conditions for regeneration. Good site preparation should minimize competition for light, water, and nutrients without causing soil loss or damage. In the context of planting, the primary goals of site preparation are to reduce competing vegetation and create conditions conducive to planting. This may, at times, be achieved simply through full-tree harvesting. Spot site preparation practices may also prove adequate, particularly for fill planting.

Mechanical, chemical, and prescribed burning treatments may be used for site preparation. Typical site preparation practices in the Lake States include disk trenching, roller chopping, scalping, and prescribed burning. Former practices that were once common include Brakee plowing and brush raking. Generally, the higher the site quality the greater the need to control woody and nonwoody vegetation to favor red pine establishment.

Herbicides work well to control competition and release planted red pine seedlings. A variety of chemicals may be used, depending on site quality, soil conditions, and competing vegetation. All herbicides must be applied by a State-certified or licensed applicator. The herbicide label includes directions, requirements for protective equipment, application site restrictions, crop species recommendations, and weed species controlled. The herbicide label instructions must be adhered to.

Prescribed burning is most effective for site preparation soon after harvesting when slash provides fuel. Conifer slash can be burned almost immediately after harvest, but hardwood slash needs several weeks to cure. In mature red pine stands, one or more summer fires can be used to eliminate shrubs and reduce duff levels before harvesting. There may be concerns about charring standing timber. Burning plans should be approved and permits obtained as required.

Planting

Planting of bare root red pine or containerized seedlings should be done in the spring. Trees should be planted at least as deep as they grew in the nursery. On drier sites, planting slightly deeper may be beneficial, but planting too deep increases risk of injury by root collar weevils. Larger bare root seedlings or transplant stock should be used on more difficult sites, or when higher probability of establishment success (but greater cost) is desired. The cost of producing containerized seedlings has been reduced in recent years and their usage has expanded. Containerized seedlings, which are preferred on sites having shallow soils, can extend the planting season into early summer.

The time required for planted red pine to reach pole size (5 inches diameter) will vary from 15 to 30 or more years depending on spacing and to a lesser extent on site quality. Closer spacings will require precommercial thinning of saplings (2-5 inches average diameter) to provide a recommended 50 square feet of growing space for each crop tree; wider spacings may need an extra release or two to control grass, shrub, and hardwood competition.

Spacing recommendations depend on many factors, including planting conditions, management objectives, and the desired final product. Planting 400 trees per acre (slightly more than a 10 x 10 foot spacing) will be less costly than closer spacing, and commercial thinnings can be made by the time trees need more growing space. Crop trees will grow rapidly, and crown closure will not shade out ground vegetation for about 20 years. Planting 800 trees per acre (a little less than 8 x 8 foot spacing) will allow greater flexibility in selecting crop trees and controlling early stand development. Crop trees will have less taper and smaller branches, and the stand will have more total volume in smaller diameter trees.

Trees should be planted at spacings of up to 10 x 10 feet if all or most of the planted trees have a good chance of surviving, precommercial thinnings are not likely, and favoring ground layer plant communities is an objective. Most production-oriented plantations are established at spacings of 6 x 8 feet and 6 x 10 feet. Machine planting costs can be reduced by using wider rows and closer spacing of trees in a row, but access for future management operations must also be considered at the time of stand establishment.

Patterns other than uniformly spaced row plantings should be considered for some extensive management and restoration applications. While planting remains a cost effective way of ensuring adequate red pine regeneration, some objectives require planted stands to look less like plantations and more like natural stands. Variable row widths and spacings or spiral planting schemes can be considered. Planting schemes can also be designed to accommodate future thinnings and harvest. For example, a rectangular 8 x 12 foot spacing would facilitate the use of modern harvesting equipment.

Seeding

Natural seeding during good seed years can successfully establish seedlings on prepared seedbeds, such as those treated with summer prescribed burning under a mature stand. Scarifying the soil may also be successful if shrubs are not present.

Direct seeding is not widely employed, but has been used successfully on well-prepared sites provided adequate soil moisture is present during the first several months after germination. Seed should be coated with bird and rodent repellants and sown at approximately 15,000 viable seeds per acre (about 5 ounces) early in spring to take advantage of moist soil conditions. Somewhat better results have been obtained by covering red pine seed with 0.25 inches of soil (it is easier to cover the seed when sowing 5 to 10 seeds in prepared spots). However, it may be easier to broadcast more seed on the surface than to use less seed and cover it. Direct seeding in general has not been successful because of inadequate site preparation, inadequate moisture, or loss of seeds to birds or rodents. There is also less control of stocking following direct seeding.

Regenerating Species Mixtures

Production managers may wish to regenerate red pine exclusively and prevent establishment of other tree species during early stand development. In contrast, extensive and reserve management may dictate regeneration of other tree species along with red pine (see Managing Red Pine Stands for Ecological Complexity). Associated species may develop from advance regeneration in the new stand through vegetative means or from seed during early stand development. Alternatively, other species may be planted along with red pine.

Releasing Regeneration

Release of red pine seedlings from shrubs and other low competitors may be needed after the third growing season. The most practical tool for release is chemical control with broadcast foliar herbicides. For best results, spraying should occur after pine leader growth is complete and the terminal bud is set, around mid-July, and be completed before the end of the growing season to avoid damage to red pine seedlings.

At the time of this writing, herbicide use is restricted on national forests in the Lake States and Northeast to nonforestry applications. Moreover, some landowners may choose not to use herbicides for a variety of reasons. In these cases, mechanical release is the only alternative. Cutting or mowing is labor intensive and results in resprouting of undesired vegetation because the root systems remain intact. It must be reapplied at 2- to 3-year intervals. Additionally, mechanical release does little to provide adequate growing space for newly planted trees on sites with abundant herbaceous competition.

A Decision Key Specific to Red Pine Regeneration

The following key (table 6) to planting and vegetation management is based on more than 30 years of combined field experience in Itasca, St. Louis, and Cook Counties in northern Minnesota. In other regions, managers may wish to make adjustments based on field experience. Nonetheless, it serves as a useful guide to managing red pine for a variety of objectives.

Consider the following when using this key:

1. Stockability refers to the stocking potential of a site in terms of suitable planting area. For example, shallow soils, exposed bedrock, and small wetlands—all common in the northern Lake States—preclude high levels of stocking.

2. The guidelines listed are intended to maximize survival of planted stock. High- intensity or production management indicates a primary goal of maximum fiber and wood production in a plantation setting. Low-intensity or extensive management implies a combination of goals, including mixed-species management.

3. Definitions:

   Delay—delay treatment in the next growing season.

   Reassess—re-evaluate during the next growing season.

   Release—remove undesirable species.

   Weed—remove competition of all sizes.

   Liberate—remove individuals overtopping desirable species.

   Fill plant—add to existing stocking by interplanting.

   Replant—ignore existing seedlings and begin stand over.

Table 6.—A decision key specific to red pine regeneration

Start	Condition or Goal	Go to or do
	Production Management	
1.	Stockability high (potential > 500-750 TPA)	2.
1.	Stockability low (potential < 500-750 TPA)	16.
2.	Age < 2 yrs in the ground	3.
2.	Age > 2 yrs in the ground	10.
3.	High fertility site	4.
3.	Low fertility site	8.
4.	Survival > 65-75%	5.
4.	Survival < 65-75%	Release and fill plant with red pine
5.	Competition is predominantly herbaceous	6.
5.	Competition is predominantly woody	7.
6.	30% trees overtopped	Release
6.	< 20-30% trees overtopped	Reassess at 5 years
7.	25% trees overtopped	Release
7.	< 10-25% trees overtopped	Reassess at 5 years
8.	Survival > 65-80%	9.
8.	Survival < 65-80%	Release and fill plant with red pine
9.	> 20-25% trees overtopped from herbaceous and woody	Release for major competition type

(Table 6 continued on next page)

(Table 6 continued)

Start	Condition or Goal	Go to or do
9.	< 20-25% of trees overtopped from herbaceous and woody	*Delay release and reassess*
10.	Survival > 60-70%	11.
10.	Survival < 60-70%	*Site preparation and replant*
11.	Competition is predominantly herbaceous	12.
11.	Competition is predominantly woody	13.
12.	> 20-40% overtopped	*Release*
12.	< 20-40% overtopped	*Reassess at 5 years*
13.	Woody species desirable in final stand	14.
13.	Woody species not desirable in final stand	15.
14.	> 10-25% overtopped	*Release*
14.	< 10-25% overtopped	*Reassess in 5 years*
15.	> 10-20% overtopped	*Release*
15.	< 10-20% overtopped	*Reassess in 2 years*
16.	Age < 2 years	17.
16.	Age > 2 years	25.
17.	High fertility site	18.
17.	Low fertility site	22.
18.	Survival > 50-70%	19.
18.	Survival < 50-70%	*Release and fill plant with red pine*
19.	Competition is predominantly herbaceous	20.
19.	Competition is predominantly woody	21.
20.	> 20-30% trees overtopped	*Release*
20.	< 20-30% trees overtopped	*Reassess in 5 years*
21.	> 10-25% trees overtopped	*Release*
21.	< 10-25% trees overtopped	*Reassess in 2 years*
22.	Survival > 50-70%	23.
22.	Survival < 50-70%	24.
23.	Grass and undesirable shrubs > 20-30%	*Release*
23.	Grass and undesirable shrubs < 20-30%	*Reassess in 5 years*
24.	Red pine and other desirable woody tree species increases density to 600 TPA	*Consider mixed-species management*
24.	Undesirable woody competition	*Release and interplant (consider inter planting with alternate species)*
25.	Survival > 40-60%	26.
25.	Survival < 40-60%	27.

(Table 6 continued on next page)

(Table 6 continued)

Start	Condition or Goal	Go to or do
	26. Grass and shrub competition overtop > 10-30% of trees	*Release*
	26. Grass and shrub competition overtop < 10-30% of trees	*Reassess in 5 years*
27.	Planted trees plus other desirable tree species density > 350-500 TPA	*Liberate planted trees*
27.	Insufficient volunteers to reach 350-500 total TPA	*Site prep and replant red pine*
	Extensive Management	
1.	Age < 3 years	2.
1.	Age > 3 years	11.
	2. Survival > 50-65%	3.
	2. Survival < 50-65%	8.
3.	Competition is predominantly herbaceous	4.
3.	Competition is predominantly woody	5.
	4. > 20-35% trees overtopped	*Spot or broadcast release*
	4. < 20-35% trees overtopped	*Assess shrub competition and monitor*
5.	Woody competition is predominantly desirable tree species	6.
5.	Woody competition is shrubs or undesirable species	7.
	6. > 25-35% trees overtopped	*Release or liberate by mechanical means*
	6. < 25-35% trees overtopped	*Monitor*
7.	> 15-25% trees overtopped	*Release or liberate by mechanical means*
7.	< 15% trees overtopped	*Monitor*
	8. Other desirable tree species > 1,000 stems per acre	9.
	8. Other desirable tree species < 500 stems per acre	10.
9.	> 25-50% planted trees overtopped by competition	*Spot release*
9.	< 25-50% planted trees overtopped	*Monitor*
	10. > 15-25% planted trees overtopped	*Patch or row scarify and fill plant (consider shade-tolerant species)*
	10. < 15-25% planted trees overtopped	*Release or liberate by mechanical means*
11.	Woody competition is predominantly desirable species	12.
11.	Woody competition is predominantly undesirable species	13.
	12. > 15-30% trees overtopped	*Release*
	12. < 15-30% trees overtopped	*Monitor*
13.	Survival > 35-65%	14.
13.	Survival < 15-35 %	*Consider site preparation and replant or fill plant*
	14. > 15-30% trees overtopped	*Release*
	14. < 15-30% trees overtopped	*Monitor*

MANAGING ESTABLISHED STANDS

Stand Density

Foresters manage stands to meet a variety of landowner objectives. In cases where timber production is the primary goal, management often focuses on maximizing financial return. This usually means encouraging growth on desirable trees while removing and utilizing the less vigorous ones. Density control is the primary means by which this is accomplished.

Stocking level and uniformity are important aspects of stand density in even-aged stands. As stocking level decreases towards a minimum, uniform distribution of trees increases in importance. Benzie (1977) calculated the minimum stocking in basal area and trees for perfectly uniform stands of various average stand diameters from the maximum amount of growing space trees of each diameter could use (fig. 2). Minimum stocking for stands averaging 5 inches in diameter is about 400 trees and 60 ft^2 per acre^{-1}. In stands averaging 15 inches in diameter, minimum stocking is about 80 trees and 100 ft^2 per acre^{-1}.

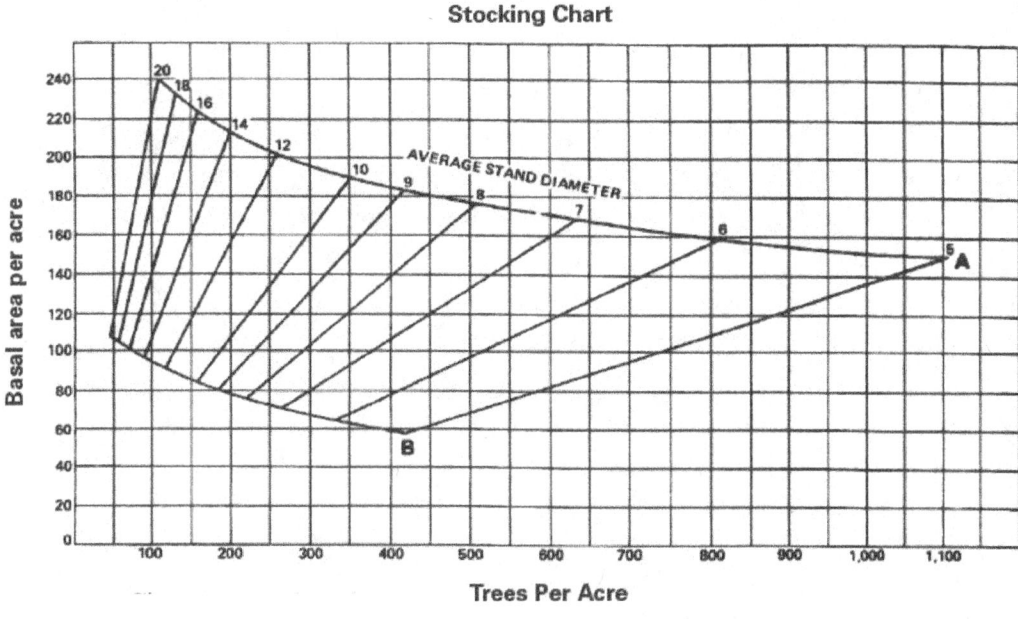

Stocking Chart

Figure 2.— Stocking chart for red pine (Benzie 1977).

The stocking chart (fig. 2) suggests the upper limit of stocking, as determined by the A-line, stands averaging 5 inches in diameter is about 1,100 trees and 150 ft^2 per acre^{-1} of basal area. For stands averaging 15 inches in diameter, the recommended upper limit of stocking is 175 trees and 215 ft^2 per acre^{-1} of basal area. Contemporary management entails lower planting densities, planting equipment considerations, and access for precommercial thinnings.

Seedling and sapling stands (less than 5 inches average diameter) should have between 400 and 900 trees per acre. Fewer than 400 trees will not provide minimum recommended stocking by the time the stand reaches poletimber size, and more than 900 trees will exceed the upper limit of recommended stocking before the trees reach poletimber size and can be thinned commercially.

Stand density guides for uneven-aged red pine stands have not been formalized. However, uneven-aged management of red pine is not uncommon. Therefore, seedlings generally need to outnumber saplings, saplings need to outnumber poles, and poles need to outnumber saw-timber trees. Losses in the smaller size classes are expected and considerable effort will be needed to ensure survival and growth of enough trees in each class to replace those harvested, lost, or recruited into the next size class. Regeneration in uneven-aged red pine stands must be monitored for Diplodia and Sirococcus shoot blights (see page 42).

Precommercial Thinning

Precommercial thinning may be needed in young stands to meet management objectives. For example, in a naturally regenerated stand of small saplings (less than 2 inches average diameter) having more than 2,000 trees per acre, a minimum of 100 potential crop trees per acre should be given a minimum growing space of 25 ft^2 per tree. Densely stocked sapling stands (2 to 5 inches average diameter) with a basal area of 160 ft^2 per acre^{-1} or more should be precommercially thinned. Crop trees in sapling stands should be given about 50 ft^2 of growing space per tree to maintain good diameter growth.

Commercial Thinning

One of the most important ways stand composition and development can be controlled is by periodic commercial thinnings. Stands should be thinned before they exceed the recommended upper limit of stocking for managed stands (see below). For production management, a uniform distribution of high-quality trees with at least the minimum recommended stocking for the average stand diameter should be left, but not over half—and preferably less—of the basal area should be removed in any one thinning. Stands managed near the minimum recommended stocking will have the most rapid diameter growth. As a general guide, pole stands (5 to 9 inches average diameter) should be thinned when basal area reaches 140 ft^2 or more per acre, leaving about 90-110 ft^2 per acre^{-1}.

Stocking charts and density management diagrams (DMDs) are popular tools for developing thinning prescriptions for even-aged stands. Their popularity stems from their ability to easily incorporate the ecological principle of self-thinning, or competition-induced mortality, which provides the stimulus for thinning. Managers should strive to prevent stands from reaching the density where self-thinning can occur. In the stocking chart (fig. 2), self-thinning begins at the A-line. Basal area is represented by the "Y" axis and trees per acre are represented by the "X" axis. Average stand diameter at breast height is represented by the lines radiating out from the origin of the two axes. Red pine stands are overstocked above the A line—too much basal area and too many trees per acre. The stand is understocked below the B line—too few trees of any size.

Stocking charts and DMDs are similar management tools, but they use a different scale of measurement (DMDs use a logarithmic scale). A density management diagram for red pine and instructions for its use can be found at:
http://www.cnr.umn.edu/FR/publications/staffpapers/Staffpaper158.pdf.

Thinning will not usually result in an increase in stand volume at the end of the rotation. Rather, it will allow individual trees to grow larger, increasing the relative rate of stand growth. Thinned volume plus volume at the end of the rotation (total yield) may or may not be higher than the total volume of an unthinned stand. Thinning, however, serves to capture volume otherwise lost to mortality. Thus, total volume removed over the life of a stand may be greater with thinning. Site quality, thinning intensity, and stand age at thinning all affect volume removed during thinning and stand volume at the end of a rotation. Residual trees should have a live crown ratio of 30 percent or greater to receive the maximum potential growth response from thinning. Many organizations emphasize a 40 percent live crown ratio. Depending on stand age, trees with shorter live crown ratios may have a minimal growth response from thinning. Red pine crowns develop upward and outward, never downward. Thus, if a stand is near its maximum potential height and has a 10 percent live crown ratio, very little growth response to thinning can be expected. For red pine, post-thinning stand density has a greater impact on post-thinning stand growth (Gilmore *et al.* 2005) than the thinning method used (Smith 2003).

For production and extensive management objectives, sawtimber trees should be thinned periodically to maintain uniform growth rates on the crop trees. For extensive management in mixed-species stands, red pine might be favored as crop trees at each thinning. However, other species should be left to achieve biodiversity goals, meet habitat requirements, and expand the species and type of timber products.

Prescribed Surface Fires

Prior to effective fire suppression, forests dominated by red pine periodically burned. Infrequent, high-intensity fires that killed overstory trees opened the canopy, exposed mineral seedbeds, facilitated regeneration, and created complex stands (see Managing Red Pine Stands for Ecological Complexity 23 p.). More frequent, low-intensity surface fires helped to thin dense stands and suppressed woody shrubs, including hazel.

Prescribed surface fire in mature red pine stands can be an effective management tool for eliminating shrub competition, reducing thick duff layers, and preparing mineral seedbeds. Summer fires, conducted over several growing seasons, are most effective at controlling dense shrub competition and exposing mineral soil. This may be done before harvesting to prepare seedbeds, unless charred bark on harvested trees poses a problem. Burning plans should be approved and permits obtained as required.

Pruning

Production managers may use pruning to increase the value of red pine sawtimber by promoting growth of clear, knot-free wood in the first log of the tree. Managers must generally balance the cost of producing high-value red pine logs containing clear wood with the costs of pruning. Pruning in concert with thinning will reduce costs and help stimulate diameter growth.

The simplest and least expensive way to prune red pine in plantations is to plant at high densities and allow trees to self-prune. Higher plantation densities also encourage straight boles with minimal taper. The natural process of pruning usually occurs as crowns close and lower branches are shaded and fall off. Artificial pruning accelerates this process. The importance of pruning has taken on greater importance with the increased use of "flitch" technology, a process in which veneer is acquired from slicing very thin boards. It generally takes about 60 years (depending on site quality, timing of pruning, and adequate thinning) to recoup the cost of pruning.

The use of proper technique is critical when pruning. Done improperly, pruning is a waste of resources and can injure trees. There are a number of things to consider when pruning red pine. Season is important; red pine pruning should be done in late fall to early spring, otherwise the bark is loose and can easily be stripped away from the stem by the weight of the branch or saw. An adequate live crown can be maintained by keeping at least the upper two-thirds of the live crown and removing only dead branches in the upper half of the tree. All dead branches should be removed. Branches should be pruned flush with the end of the branch collar so no stub remains (stubs can be entry sites for insect and disease infestations). Only the largest diameter (dominant and codominant) trees with the best form should be pruned because these trees have the greatest potential for return on investment. Pruning should begin when trees reach a d.b.h. of 4 to 6 inches, and those with numerous branches greater than 2 inches in diameter should be avoided.

Pruning may also be important in extensive management when objectives include production of large quantities of trees with high-quality, knot-free timber. Moreover, pruning promotes development of clear boles, which can be characteristic of old-growth conditions. Because spacing in stands managed less intensively is typically wider than that in uniform plantations, pruning may be required to remove lower branches on potentially high-value trees.

In mixed-species stands, we recommend pruning if the stand is dominated by the desired species (more than 60 percent of the trees). However, look for the possibility of an exchange of dominance whereby unpruned trees overtake and reduce the growth of pruned trees in the years immediately following pruning. In such cases, pruning all stems in the stand may be the best course of action.

Growth and Yield

Growth and yield equations have been refined over the years, but for the most part "modern" equations do not differ greatly from volume tables published in the early 1900s. Stand volume and individual tree prediction equations are provided in appendix B (table B2). Basal area growth and yield tables from Benzie (1977) and derived from the works of Buckman (1962) are presented in tables B2 through B8 in appendix B.

Rotation Age

Many factors determine rotation age, including site quality, desired product, stocking, and management intensity. Generally, for production management purposes, the rotation age for red pine is between 60 to 90 years, as defined by culmination of mean annual volume growth increment. However, red pine is a long-lived species, providing opportunities to grow and manage stands for up to 200 years and individual trees to even greater ages. In fact, rotations exceeding 100 to 150 years have become more common on public lands and when managing for large-diameter sawtimber. Periodic thinning extends economic rotation age by delaying culmination of mean annual increment. Rotation ages based on maximum mean annual boardfoot growth at different levels of basal area (after periodic thinning) are provided in table C1 of appendix C.

For reserve and extensive management, declining growth rates in older stands are not a primary concern. Rather, the ecological contributions of old trees and stands are of primary interest. Consequently, the shape of the mean annual increment curve and the influence of thinning on growth may be less important to these landowners.

MANAGING RED PINE STANDS FOR ECOLOGICAL COMPLEXITY

Ecological complexity in forest stands takes many forms—for example, species diversity, a wide range of tree ages and sizes, multiple age cohorts, snags and dead logs on the ground, cavity trees, wolf trees, tip-up pits and mounds, characteristic understory plant communities, and varying forest floor conditions and soil patterns. Complex stands also vary in structure and composition spatially, compared with simplified stands that are often uniform throughout. The sustainability of native species (one aspect of biological diversity) often depends on the availability of structures and on the heterogeneity that exists in complex forest stands.

Forest managers have little experience with managing red pine stands for complex stand conditions. There are no quantitative guidelines for doing so. However, such complexity was the rule, not the exception before European-settlement. For example, evidence in the Lake States indicates that red pine stands often included several other species in moderate abundance including eastern white pine, jack pine, paper birch, aspen, oaks, and maples. Moreover, older pine stands dominated the landscape, with up to 30 percent of them greater than 120 years old. A reference stand exhibiting these characteristics exists in the "Lost Forty" in northern Minnesota. Also, the age range of red pine in such stands sometimes spanned 100 years. Historical photographs of red pine stands show the presence of snags, multiple species, and several age cohorts; stand density, tree size, and tree condition vary, as do the distribution of regeneration in the understory.

This is not to say that all presettlement red pine stands were highly complex; indeed, a range of variation likely existed. Some stands dominated by red pine no doubt were largely single-aged, but even they were more complex than most managed stands in the contemporary landscape (e.g., they contained some snags and trees of other species). Today's managed red pine stands, by comparison, tend to be highly simplified in composition, age structure, density of snags, logs, etc. It is also worth noting that stand complexity is not strictly a feature of old stands. Even young stands regenerating after natural disturbances contain some larger, residual trees, as well as abundant snags and logs on the ground and patches of undisturbed understory vegetation and forest floor (fig. 3).

Figure 3.—

Simple versus ecologically complex young red pine stands; complex stands may include large residual trees from the previous stand, including species other than red pine, snags, and dead logs on the ground.

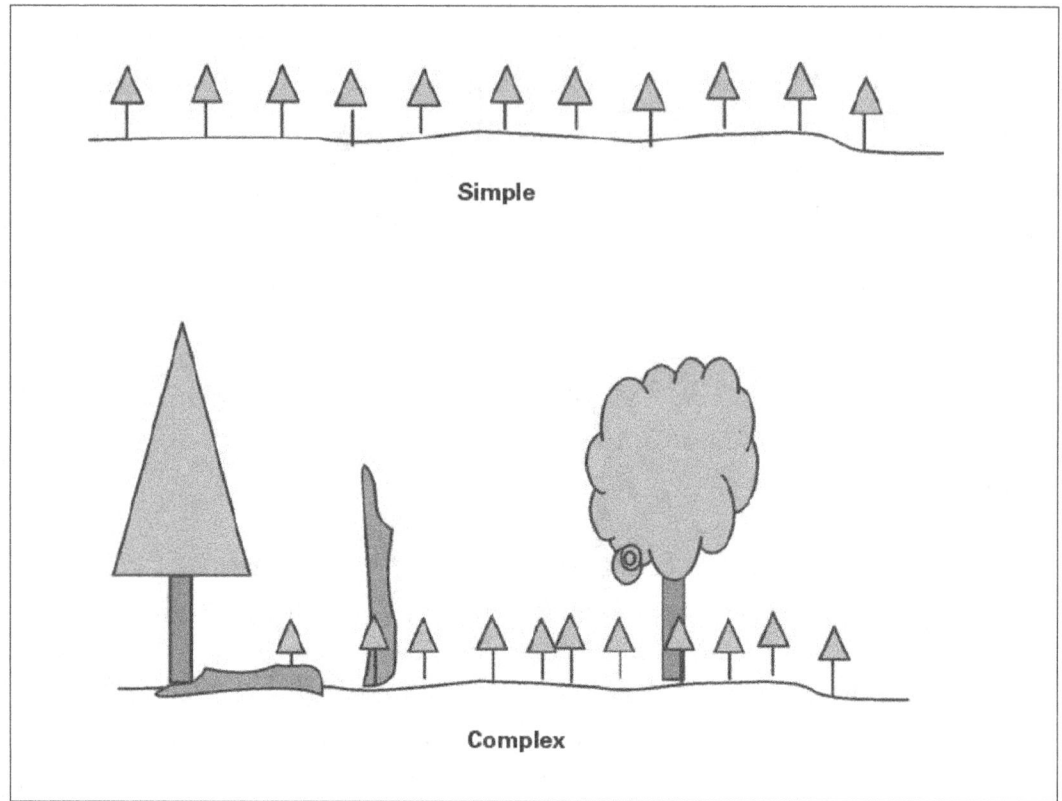

INCORPORATING ECOLOGICAL COMPLEXITY INTO RED PINE MANAGEMENT

Although managing red pine stands for ecological complexity is usually not a goal of production management, it can certainly be an issue in ecological reserves and also in extensive management. In addition to the general tools and approaches for red pine management outlined in this guide, the following basic principles should be considered when designing an approach to sustain or restore ecological complexity:

1) Incorporate biological legacies into regeneration harvest prescriptions.

2) Incorporate natural stand development processes into intermediate treatments.

3) Allow appropriate recovery periods between regeneration harvests.

Incorporate Biological Legacies into Harvesting Prescriptions

Biological legacies.—Biological legacies are the organisms, structures, and biologically created patterns that persist from the predisturbance forest and influence development in the postdisturbance stand (table 7). Structural legacies include large, healthy, live trees, decadent trees, snags, and logs and other coarse woody debris on the forest floor. Compositional legacies include the organisms that survive a disturbance—trees, of course, but also nonarboreal plants, fungi, and animals. Legacy patterns include the spatial distribution of remnant patches of undisturbed understory vegetation, forest floor, and mineral soil.

Table 7.—Categories of biological legacies with some examples of types

Legacy category	Examples
Organisms	Mature, healthy live trees; declining trees Tree reproduction Seed banks Shrub, herb, bryophyte species Mature and immature animals
Organic matter	Fine litter, particulate material
Organically derived structures	Standing dead trees Downed trees, coarse woody debris Root wads and pits from uprooted trees
Organically derived patterns	Soil chemical, physical, microbial properties Forest understory composition and distribution

Modifying traditional regeneration harvests.—Traditional clearcut regeneration prescriptions should be modified to include retention of large (healthy) red pine trees (and other species if they are present), decadent trees, snags, and downed logs in a variety of sizes, including large stems. Special consideration should be given to actual or potential cavity trees, mast trees, and nest trees. Natural regeneration should be protected and promoted whenever possible, along with planting or direct seeding.

Red pine shoot blight.—If red pine shoot blight is a concern (see Damaging Agents, p. 29), consider regenerating primarily white and jack pine after an initial regeneration harvest (or red pine in areas where no evidence of shoot blight exists). Reducing losses from shoot blight while retaining significant numbers of overstory red pine may mean retaining overstory red pine during an initial regeneration harvest, then planting or seeding other species (primarily white and/or jack pine). Then, at the end of the next rotation, primarily mature white and jack pine can be retained during a regeneration harvest, followed by planting or seeding of red pine.

Retaining structure.—Determining the number and distribution of live trees, snags, logs, and other structural elements will depend on management objectives and desired future conditions. For instance, retention of low numbers of residual red pine (e.g., 20-30 ft²/acre), followed by regeneration, will result in largely single age-cohort stands containing scattered older trees. In contrast, retention of 60-80 ft² per acre of residual red pine at an initial harvest will result in the development of two-age cohort stands and potentially multi-cohort stands if this level of retention is repeated at future harvests. Leaving even small amounts of residual trees may result in an overall reduction in growth of regeneration, but the continued growth of the residual trees may well compensate for growth loss in the new cohort. Some ecological objectives are best achieved by dispersing trees, snags, and other structures throughout the stand, while others are best served by leaving patches of legacy trees (fig. 4, table 8). Best results may be obtained by alternating between patch and dispersed cutting across the harvest unit. Retaining some large aggregates of live trees is also a good way to protect understory plant communities and forest floor environments. It may be best to adapt species regeneration to residual overstory conditions—for example, favoring white pine under dispersed retention and red or jack pine in openings.

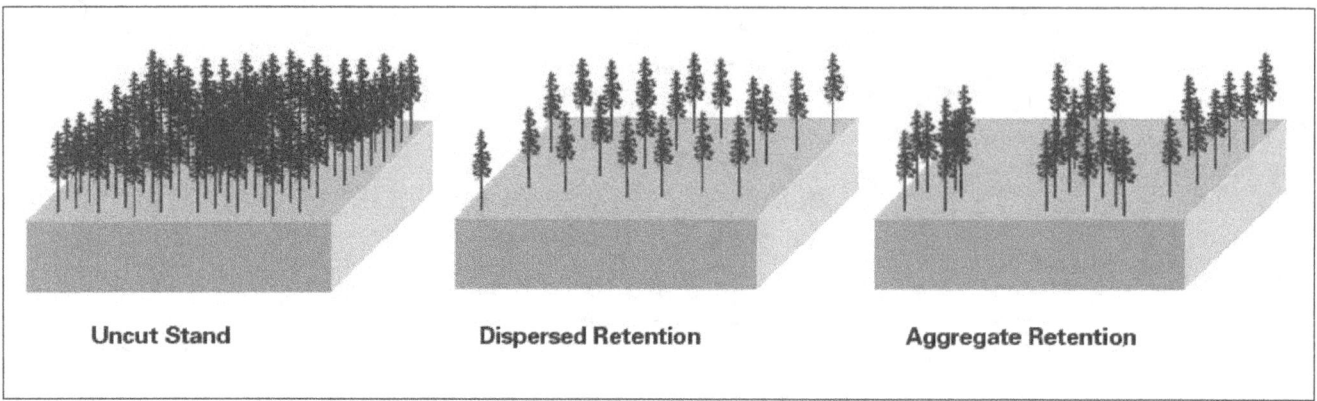

Figure 4.—Differing spatial patterns of red pine retention after a regeneration harvest.

Table 8.—Effects of live tree retention pattern on red pine ecosystem characteristics

Characteristic	Dispersed	Aggregate
Regeneration growth (intolerant species)	Lower	Higher (between aggregates)
Regeneration growth (tolerant species)	Higher	Lower (outcompeted between aggregates)
Hazel production	Higher	Lower
Blueberry production	Lower	Higher
Logging efficiency	Lower	Higher
Residual tree damage	Higher	Lower
Campground quality	Lower	Higher
Fuels distribution	Uniform	Aggregate
Tree form and geometry	Uniform	Variable

Incorporate Natural Stand Development Processes into Intermediate Treatments

Intermediate stand treatments such as thinning and pruning mimic the natural processes of tree mortality and decline. In application, traditional thinning and pruning regimes create spatially uniform stands. Ecological complexity can be increased in established red pine stands by modifying traditional intermediate treatments and adding nontraditional approaches like "decadence creation". In addition to "decadence creation", specific treatments include variable density thinning, maintaining or improving species diversity, and prescribed burning.

Variable density thinning.—In traditional applications, stands are thinned uniformly to provide crop trees with equal access to moisture, nutrients, and light. In contrast, most unmanaged forests have varying stand density and a wider range of tree growth rates and sizes. In such stands, mortality from competition, along with wind, lightning, insects, or fire can cause mortality during stand development. To emulate this natural variation, managers can apply different degrees of thinning throughout the stand—i.e., some areas can be thinned heavily, some moderately, and some left unthinned (fig. 5). This will result in variable stand density and greater structural diversity.

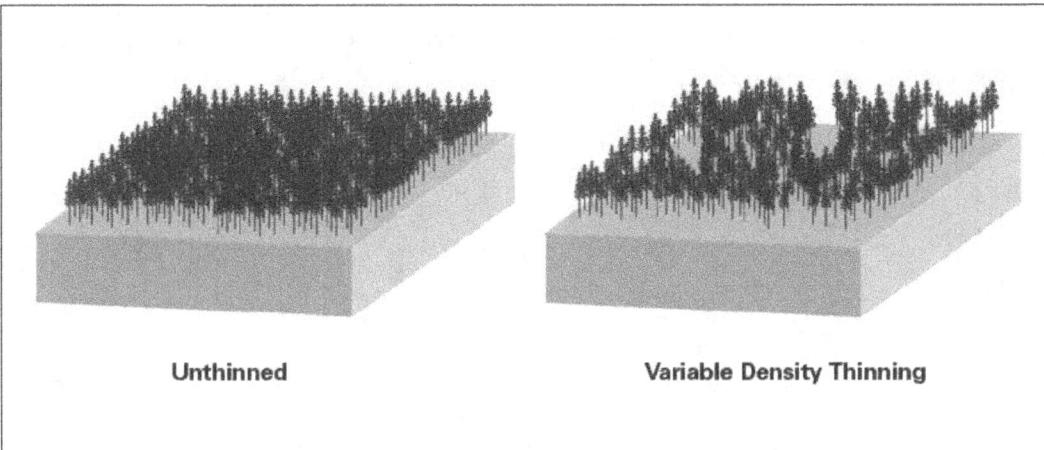

Unthinned   **Variable Density Thinning**

Figure 5.— Conceptual representation of variable density thinning in a red pine stand, including gaps, unthinned areas, and varying levels of thinning between these extremes.

Decadence creation.—Consider deliberate felling of live trees to increase the abundance and types of dead logs on the ground. Also, consider girdling (or killing in some other way) living trees to create snags. A range of tree sizes should be considered, including large diameter red pine individuals.

Improving species diversity.—Leaving some large gaps during thinning should help promote less shade-tolerant tree, shrub, and herbaceous species. These species should be encouraged for their contributions to ecological complexity and native plant diversity. Thinning should not preferentially remove non-target tree species, that is, species other than red pine. In particular, noncommercial species should be retained for their contributions to ecological complexity and biological diversity. Finally, consider underplanting tolerant species, where seed sources or advance regeneration for these are lacking.

Prescribed burning.—As mentioned earlier, surface fires periodically swept through red pine forests, particularly on drier sites. Reintroducing surface fires will help maintain (or restore) understory conditions that reflect those existing prior to effective fire suppression. Fires should be allowed to burn naturally across the stand—that is, without making an effort to ensure that the stand burns evenly. Surface fires will improve ecological diversity through fire scarring and small-scale canopy disturbance if individual trees are killed. Care should be taken not to burn under extremely dry conditions, as excessive injury or mortality may result.

Allow Appropriate Recovery Periods Between Regeneration Harvests

Allowing appropriate recovery periods between regeneration harvests will aid development of structural and compositional complexity in red pine stands. Traditionally, red pine stands are harvested before significant complexity has developed (fig. 6), a problem compounded when stands are deliberately or inadvertently simplified during establishment.

In general, economic rotation age is linked to culmination of mean annual increment; this occurs somewhere between 50 and 90 years in unthinned red pine. If ecological complexity is a primary goal, there is little reason to base rotation age for such a long-lived species only on growth and economic factors. Rather, stands should be allowed to develop sufficient structural and compositional complexity and spatial heterogeneity, a process that can be accelerated with appropriate intermediate treatments.

Figure 6.— Development of ecological complexity in a red pine stand over time.

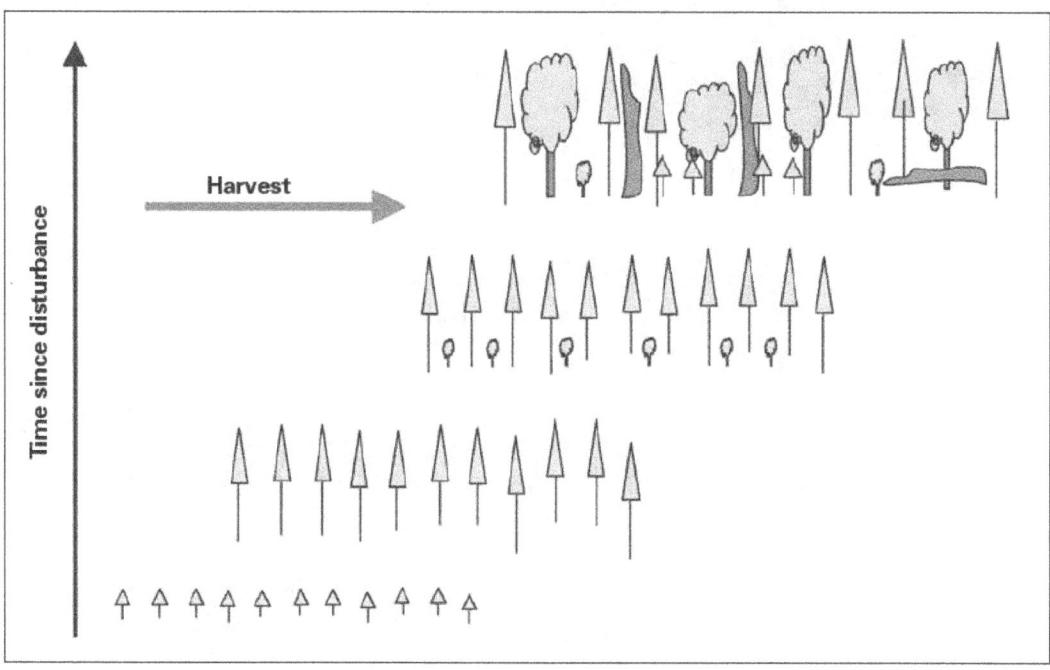

Damaging Agents

Due to its limited genetic diversity, red pine does not demonstrate much disease resistance. Yet it is often used in reforestation because it has fewer damaging agents than other species. Nonetheless, red pine can be damaged or killed by several diseases (table 9). Periodic outbreaks of these diseases, which typically affect young trees, can cause planting failures or reduced productivity of established plantations.

Table 9.—Major red pine pathogens and tree classes affected

Pathogen	Disease	Tree class
Gremmeniella abietina	Canker	Seedling-sapling
Diplodia pinea	Shoot blight, collar rot, and canker	Seedling-pole
Sirococcus conigenus	Shoot blight	Seedling-sapling
Lophodermium seditiosum	Needle cast	Seedling-sapling
Coleosporium asterum	Needle rust	Seedling-sapling
Armillaria spp.	Root and butt rot	Seedling-pole
Heterobasidion annosum	Root and butt rot	Sapling-mature
Phellinus pini	Trunk rot	Mature
Inonotus tomentosus	Root and butt rot	Mature

Insect pests can work in concert with pathogens to further stress trees and increase their vulnerability to damage. To avoid this, it is important to recognize potential disease problems and the risks they represent before planting trees or applying silvicultural treatments.

Fortunately, it is often possible to reduce disease risk and minimize losses by establishing red pine plantings on appropriate sites, timing silvicultural treatments to maintain high tree vigor, and detecting and controlling insect and disease outbreaks as soon as possible. Managers should emphasize long-term strategies that prevent or reduce the risk of disease outbreaks in current as well as in future stands (table 10).

MAJOR DISEASES OF RED PINE

Illustrated publications to assist in the identification of the following red pine diseases, including descriptions of pathogen life cycles and management suggestions, are available online at the following Web site and related links: http://na.fs.us/spfo/ and http://ncrs.fs.fed.us/.

Table 10.—Guidelines to reduce or prevent the risk of disease outbreaks

Disease	Proper site selection	Plant healthy stock	Control competing vegetation	Sanitation	Avoid wounding	Pruning
Control strategies						
Gremmeniella canker	X	X		X		X
Diplodia canker	X	X	X		X	
Sirococcus shoot blight	X			X		X
Armillaria root rot	X					
Lophodermium needle cast	X	X				
Needle rust	X		X			
Heterobasidion root rot				X	X	
Phellinus trunk rot					X	
Inonotus root rot	X					

Shoot Blight and Canker Diseases

Scleroderris canker.—Scleroderris canker, caused by the fungus *Gremmeniella abietina*, affects primarily young trees, and seldom damages trees taller than 2 m. Because the disease develops on lower branches under snow cover, it causes the most problems in frost pockets and areas that receive deep snow. Planting red pine on sites favorable for disease development and inadvertently planting infected nursery stock have resulted in this disease becoming a major problem in the Lake States and Northeastern States.

The Scleroderris fungus spreads through windblown spores (ascospores) that infect buds and needles in spring, causing an orange discoloration at the base of affected needles. Infected branch tips are usually dead by the following summer. The fungus can spread from the branch into the main stem, where a canker develops that can girdle and kill young trees. The fungus produces a second spore (conidiospore) that is disseminated by rain splash from dead branches to adjacent trees, increasing the disease incidence.

Preventing damage by Scleroderris canker begins with planting disease-free nursery stock and avoiding planting sites where the fungus is already present or where frost pockets and cold air drainage make seedlings especially susceptible. Pruning the lower branches on infected and healthy trees will reduce incidence of this disease in high-value plantations.

Diplodia shoot blight and canker.—The fungus *Diplodia pinea* can cause epidemics of shoot blight and cankers on trees stressed by drought or predisposed to infection through injury or poor site conditions. The fungus causes shoot blight on large trees, shoot blight and cankers on sapling and pole-size trees, and shoot blight and collar rot on seedlings. Trees are infected through succulent shoot tissues, branch stubs, or wounds caused by thinning and harvesting, storm damage, hail, and insects. The fungus can grow from infected shoots into branch and stem wood, developing cankers that often girdle or kill the tree.

Infected residual trees and red pine windbreaks are often the sources of *D. pinea* inoculum. The fungus can invade shoot tissues and persist without causing symptoms until infected trees are stressed, at which time the disease develops rapidly. Multi-cohort management, including seed tree and shelterwood regeneration, will increase the risk of disease if overstory and adjacent reserve trees are harboring inoculum.

The risk of Sphaeropsis shoot blight and canker can be reduced by planting healthy stock obtained from nurseries known to protect seedlings from infection and by not planting red pine near infected trees in areas where the disease has previously been a problem. Since this pathogen is especially damaging to stressed trees, poor sites where soil moisture is a limiting factor should be avoided. Control of competing vegetation to maintain high tree vigor can also reduce disease impact.

Sirococcus shoot blight.—The fungus *Sirococcus conigenus* causes a shoot blight that periodically becomes epidemic in red pine plantations during extended periods of wet spring weather. It damages or kills young red pine seedlings, saplings, and shoots on older trees. Trees growing under or adjacent to infected red pine can be severely affected when conditions are optimum for fungus dissemination and development.

Spores (conidia) are released in spring and early summer. The fungus infects needles and grows into the current year's shoots. Unlike *D. pinea*, *S. conigenus* rarely enters older stem tissues, thus it is a problem on older trees only after 2 or 3 years of severe disease.

Outbreaks of Sirococcus shoot blight, like those of *Diplodia* shoot blight, are episodic and can rapidly increase. Removing infected overstory trees and pruning infected shoots on understory trees before spore dispersal in early spring will reduce the major sources of inoculum and minimize future disease incidence.

Needle Diseases

Lophodermium needle cast and Coleosporium needle rust.—Needle diseases such as Lophodermium needle cast (caused by *Lophodermium seditiosum*) and pine needle rust (caused by *Coleosporium asterum*) are often conspicuous on young trees but seldom damaging except in nurseries and Christmas tree plantings.

Pine needle rust is most severe on sites where its alternate hosts, goldenrod and aster, are abundant; in such instances, it can limit growth and even kill young trees. Needle rust can be reduced by avoiding planting on sites with goldenrod and aster unless they can be removed by mowing or use of herbicides.

Root and Butt Rots

Armillaria root rot.—Armillaria shoestring root rot, caused by several species in the fungal genus *Armillaria,* is common on stressed trees and trees weakened by insects or other diseases. Many red pine trees are probably infected with *Armillaria* but exhibit symptoms only when stressed by other biotic or abiotic factors. Fungal decay, which can extend several feet above the ground, eventually girdles trees at the root collar, creating clusters of dead and dying trees. Red pine trees growing on cutover hardwood sites are especially vulnerable, presumably because of the increased source of inoculum in roots and stumps of harvested trees.

Stunting and yellowing of infected trees are the first symptoms of disease. Mushrooms may develop at the base of infected trees in fall, producing windborne spores that can spread the fungus.

The incidence of Armillaria root and butt rot in red pine stands can be reduced by maintaining high tree vigor. Planting on sites with evidence of diseased trees or with abundant hardwood stumps that may harbor the fungus should be avoided.

Annosum root and butt rot.—Like Armillaria, Annosum root and butt rot (caused by the fungus *Heterobasidion annosum*) can result in clusters of dead and dying trees. Although Annosum root rot has not been a widespread problem in red pine, it has the potential to cause damage after thinning and harvesting in some stands.

Inonotus root and butt rot.—*Inonotus tomentosus* causes a root and butt rot of mature trees, but it can also damage seedlings and young trees on sites where the fungus remains from the previous stand. It infects trees through wounded roots and root collars, developing a resinous canker. Affected trees have reduced growth and are susceptible to windthrow.

Phellinus trunk rot.—*Phellinus pini,* which causes a white pocket rot in mature trees, is sometimes called red rot because of the color of the wood in the early stages of decay. Symptoms include swollen knots, punk knots (masses of brown fungal hyphae protruding from decayed branch stubs), and brown basidiocarps (conks) on trunks of infected trees. Infection enters through wounds and broken branches. There are no effective control measures other than to avoid wounding trees.

Insect Pests of Red Pine

Although numerous insects attack red pine, only a few represent serious, persistent, or widespread threats. These are reviewed below.

Needle-Feeding Insects

Several defoliators can cause localized outbreaks in red pine that result in growth loss and occasionally, tree mortality. The redheaded pine sawfly, *Neodiprion lecontei,* is most likely to cause significant damage. The pine tussock moth, *Dasychira plagiata,* can also kill trees. Both species eat both old (previous-year) and current-year needles, completely defoliating trees. Most other defoliators found on red pine eat either old or current-year needles.

Redheaded pine sawfly outbreaks have occurred throughout the Lake States. Feeding is heaviest on young trees (less than 20 feet tall) and on sites that would be defined as stressful for red pine—that is, highly disturbed sandy areas, frost pockets, and hardwood edges.

Pine tussock moth outbreaks have occurred infrequently in the Lake States, generally in northwestern Wisconsin. Tree mortality has been reported following outbreaks.

The red pine needle midge, *Thecodiplosis piniresinosae*, feeds throughout the summer, but characteristic needle browning does not develop until late fall (see table 11). In early summer, midge larvae tunnel into the base of needle fascicles. Feeding causes premature needle mortality, referred to as fall browning or needle droop. Damage is often concentrated in the tops of young trees, where terminal shoots may be killed. Persistent midge populations tend to be associated with red pine plantations growing on poor sites.

Table 11.—Common insect pests associated with different stages of red pine plantation development

Seedlings (1-5 years)	Saplings (6-20 years)	Pole-sized (21-40 years)	Mature and old growth (41-200+ years)
White grubs	Saratoga spittlebug	*Ips* bark beetles	*Ips* bark beetles
Saratoga spittlebug	Root collar weevil	Root tip weevil	Red turpentine beetle
	European pine shoot moth	Red pine shoot moth	Red pine shoot moth
	Redheaded pine sawfly	Pine shoot beetle	Pine shoot beetle
	Red pine needle midge	Red pine needle midge	Red pine cone beetle
	Pine tussock moth	Pine tussock moth	
		Red pine cone beetle	

The Saratoga spittlebug, *Aphrophora saratogensis*, has probably been the most significant pest of young red pine across northern portions of Michigan, Minnesota, and Wisconsin. Large spittlebug populations cause extensive wounding that can kill branches and eventually entire trees. Plantation failures have been reported. High spittlebug populations are associated with abundant sweetfern, the plant that serves as a host for the insect's immature stage. Several other plants can also serve as alternate hosts including willows and raspberries/blackberries.

Root and Root-Collar Insects

White grubs are the larvae of beetles referred to as May and June beetles. They live in the soil and feed on fine roots of many plants, including young pine. They have been responsible for planting failures throughout the Lake States region. Most damage occurs when planting into existing sod.

The pine root collar weevil, *Hylobius radicis*, can be a serious pest of young (5- to 15-year-old) red pine. Larvae feed at the base of trees where they can girdle the stem or cause deformity. Heavily infested trees often break at the weakened area and tip over. Damage is associated with poorly stocked stands growing in heavy grass. Windbreak trees and trees growing along the edges of plantations are most likely to be infested. Scotch pine (*Pinus sylvestris*) is very susceptible to this weevil, and red pines growing in association with Scotch pines are more likely to be infested.

The root tip weevil, *Hylobius rhizophagus*, is most often found attacking red pine growing in close association with jack pine. Infested red pines have flagged (dead) branches and often appear stunted. The symptoms can be very similar to those resulting from Saratoga spittlebug attacks or some of the shoot pathogens.

Shoot-Mining Insects

European pine shoot moth, *Rhyacionia buoliana*, larvae feed on buds and shoots of red pine. The worst damage occurs when heavy infestation causes the top whorl to lose dominance to a branch on the lower stem. Damage tends to be corrected over time. This insect is limited to lower Michigan, southeastern Wisconsin, and a few other locations where consistently heavy snow cover provides optimum insulation for larvae during winter.

The red pine shoot moth, *Dioryctria resinosella*, can also be a significant problem. Larval feeding on shoots can result in significant height and radial growth losses.

Bark and Wood-Infesting Insects

Pine bark beetles in the genus *Ips* are associated with almost every red pine that dies. They are generally viewed as secondary pests, and rarely attack plantations younger than 25 years of age. Past that point, outbreaks are often associated with lack of thinning and drought. Outbreaks are usually limited to small groups of trees, but during periods of significant drought they can kill trees over several acres. Thinning and timber harvesting can also trigger *Ips* outbreaks; freshly cut logs greater than 1 inch in diameter left in the woods in spring and early summer can provide breeding sites for large beetle populations.

The red turpentine beetle, *Dendroctonus valens*, is a common bark beetle that attacks trees from the ground line up 3 to 4 feet. They create characteristic popcorn-like pitch tubes. These beetles are not considered tree killers but their tunnels and feeding reduce tree vigor, making infested trees susceptible to infestation by *Ips* bark beetles.

An exotic pine shoot beetle, *Tomicus piniperda*, has the potential to damage red pine stands in the Lake States. Much like the native *Ips* beetles, this European beetle lays its eggs and develops under the bark of stressed and recently killed pines. However, the adults also have a feeding stage inside the shoots of host trees. High populations can result in heavy shoot mining and significant loss of foliage.

Seed and Cone Insects

Red pine has an array of insects that attack its reproductive structures, especially developing second-year cones. The most significant of these is the red pine cone beetle, *Conophthorus resinosa*, which can cause complete cone crop failures and adversely affect natural regeneration. The greatest damage typically follows several years of high cone production. Because red pine cone beetles spend the winter on the forest floor in hollowed-out shoots, prescribed fires conducted prior to beetle emergence in the spring offer excellent control potential.

Insects and Stand Development

Susceptibility to and incidence of pest species varies with stage of stand development (table 11). Seedlings have small root systems that can easily be damaged by root-feeding insects.

In some situations, insect damage can be extensive in sapling stands prior to crown closure. Plantation failures have been documented on sites dominated by sweetfern due to infestations of Saratoga spittlebug. Many of these sites are also frost pockets.

Root collar weevil can also be a serious pest of young red pine, especially on nutrient-deficient sites. Improperly planted trees with j-roots are very susceptible, as are trees growing in heavy sod. Because scotch pine is a favored host of this weevil, its presence may increase the likelihood of attack in nearby red pine.

Defoliators like the redheaded pine sawfly and pine tussock moth can kill young trees. Localized outbreaks of redheaded pine sawfly are most often associated with either dry, nutrient-poor sites or mesic, nutrient-rich sites.

Shoot-mining insects do occur in young red pine stands but are relatively minor pests. The European pine shoot moth damages terminal buds and can distort shoot growth. However, it does not occur over most of the range of red pine in the Lake States. Red pine shoot moth attacks can begin in plantations prior to crown closure, but most outbreaks have been reported in slightly older stands. On rare occasions, white pine weevils will attack the terminal shoots of red pine.

Following crown closure, red pine pole stands are relatively immune to insect problems. Bark beetles in the genus *Ips* can kill small groups of trees, and larger groups of trees on rare occasions. *Ips* bark beetles attack trees that are weakened by poor site conditions, drought, or intense competition. Thinning stands to recommended stocking levels reduces stress and decreases the likelihood of *Ips* infestations.

The red pine shoot moth can pose a threat to plantations that are 20 to 40 years of age and growing on sandy outwash soils.

In some areas, the root tip weevil can kill pole-size pine outright. Root tip weevil is most prevalent in northwestern and central Wisconsin and the western half of the Upper Peninsula. The presence of jack pine intermixed with red pine increases the likelihood of infestations.

Older red pines have the ability to defend themselves against insects and pathogens. One study found that mature red pine trees (100 to 220 years old) have higher resin flow than younger trees, giving them a defense against bark beetles.

AVOIDING INSECT RELATED PROBLEMS

Because most insect-related problems in red pine are associated with specific site and stand conditions, managers can avoid problems by knowing what these conditions are. Planting red pine on appropriate sites will significantly reduce the likelihood of insect attacks. Managers should use ecological classification systems such as habitat type guides to identify these sites.

In addition, managers should follow these guidelines:

1) Avoid planting into heavy grass competition. Grass competes with young trees for moisture and nutrients, and existing sod can harbor high white grub populations.

2) Avoid areas dominated by sweetfern. Incidence of Saratoga spittlebug is directly related to abundance of sweetfern. If the site is already planted, eliminate the sweetfern.

3) Avoid planting in frost pockets. Recurring frost stunts growth and reduces tree vigor, making trees more susceptible to insect injury. Saratoga spittlebug damage is often concentrated in frost pockets.

4) Use healthy seedlings and plant properly. Such seedlings will develop into fast-growing young trees that are better able to withstand insect feeding than inferior seedlings.

5) Avoid mixing red pine with Scotch pine under any circumstances. Jack pine can also spread insects to red pine. White pine and some hardwoods are appropriate associates for red pine on many sites.

6) Thin red pine stands as recommended. High stand density can create competition stress, making trees more susceptible to bark beetles. Thinning is best done in late summer, fall, or early winter.

7) During spring and summer thinning operations, remove cut material larger than 4 inches within 3 weeks. Winter-harvested material should be removed before warm spring weather occurs.

References

Alban, D.H. 1972a.
An improved growth intercept method for estimating site index of red pine. Res. Pap. NC-80. St. Paul, MN: U.S. Department of Agriculture, Forest Service, North Central Forest Experiment Station. 7 p.

Alban, D.H. 1972b.
The relationship of red pine site index to soil phosphorus extracted by several methods. Soil Science Society of America Proceedings. 36(4): 664-666.

Alban, D.H. 1974.
Red pine site index in Minnesota as related to soil and foliar nutrients. Forest Science. 20: 261.

Alban, D.H. 1976.
Estimating red pine site index in northern Minnesota. Res. Pap. NC-130. St. Paul, MN: U.S. Department of Agriculture, Forest Service, North Central Forest Experiment Station. 13 p.

Benzie, J.W. 1977.
Red pine in the north-central states. Gen. Tech. Rep. NC-33. St. Paul, MN: U.S. Department of Agriculture, Forest Service, North Central Forest Experiment Station. 22 p.

Brown, J.H.; Duncan, C.A. 1990.
Site index of red pine in relation to soils and topography in the Allegheny Plateau of Ohio. Northern Journal of Applied Forestry. 7: 129-133.

Buckman, R.E. 1962.
Growth and yield of red pine in Minnesota. Tech. Bull. 1272. Washington, DC: U.S. Department of Agriculture. 50 p.

Carmean, W.H.; Hahn J.T.; Jacobs, R.D. 1989.
Site index curves for forest tree species in the eastern United States. Gen. Tech. Rep. NC-128. St. Paul, MN: U.S. Department of Agriculture, Forest Service, North Central Forest Experiment Station. 142 p.

David, A.; Pike, C.; Stine, R. 2003.
Comparison of selection methods for optimizing genetic gain and family diversity in a red pine (*Pinus resinosa* Ait.) seedlings seed orchard. Theoretical Applied Genetics. 107(5): 843-849.

Fowler, G.W. 1997.
Individual tree volume equations for red pine in Michigan. Northern Journal of Applied Forestry. 14: 53-58.

Gevorkiantz, S.R. 1957.
Site index curves for red pine in the Lake States. Tech. Note 484. St Paul, MN: U.S. Department of Agriculture, Forest Service, Lake Forest Experiment Station. 2 p.

Gilmore, A.R. 1968.
Site index curves for plantation-grown white pine in Illinois. For. Note 121. University of Illinois [Chicago, IL]: Agricultural Experiment Station. 2 p.

Gilmore, D.W.; O'Brien, T.C.; Hoganson, H.M. 2005.
Thinning red pine plantations and the Langsaeter hypothesis: a northern Minnesota case study. Northern Journal of Applied Forestry. 22: 19-26.

Hannah, P.R. 1971.
Soil-site relationships for white, Scotch, and red pine plantations in Vermont, VT: Sta. Bull. 667. University of Vermont Agricultural Experiment Station. 25 p.

Hicock, H.W.; Morgan, M.F.; Luts, H.J.; Lunt, H.A. 1931.
Relation of forest composition and rate of growth to certain soil characters. Bull. 330. CT: Connecticut Agricultural Experimental Station: 673-750.

Katovich, S.A.; Hall, D.J. 1992.
How to identify and minimize red pine shoot moth damage. NA-FR-02-92. Radnor, PA: U.S. Department of Agriculture, Forest Service, Northeastern Area, State & Private Forestry. n.p.

Lundgren, A.L.; Dolid, W.A. 1970.
Biological growth functions describe published site index curves for Lake States timber species. Res. Pap. NC-36. St. Paul, MN: U.S. Department of Agriculture, Forest Service, North Central Forest Experiment Station. 9 p.

Lundgren, A.L. 1971.
The effect of initial number of trees per acre and thinning densities on timber yields from red pine plantations in the Lake States. Res. Pap. NC-193. St. Paul, MN: U.S. Department of Agriculture, Forest Service, North Central Forest Experiment Station. 25 p.

Mack, T.J.; Burk, T.E. 2004.
Equations for predicting merchantable yield and diameter distribution for Lake States red pine. Northern Journal of Applied Forestry. 21: 107-110.

Nicholls, T.H.; Skilling, D.D. 1990.
Pocket guide to red pine diseases and their management. Misc. Publ. U.S. Department of Agriculture, Forest Service, North Central Forest Experiment Station. 41 p.

Ostry, M.E.; Nicholls, T.H.; Skilling, D.D. 1990.
Biology and control of Sirococcus shoot blight on red pine. Res. Pap. NC-295. St. Paul, MN: U.S. Department of Agriculture, Forest Service, North Central Forest Experiment Station. 11 p.

Richards, N.A.; Morrow, R.R; Stone, E.L. 1962.
Influence of soil and site on red pine plantations in New York. I. Stand development and site index curves. Bull. 977. Ithaca, NY: Cornell University Experiment Station. 24 p.

Skilling, D.D.; Schneider, B.; Fasking, D. 1986.
Biology and control of Scleroderris canker in North America. Res. Pap. NC-275. St. Paul, MN: U.S. Department of Agriculture, Forest Service, North Central Forest Experiment Station. 18 p.

Smith, D.M. 2003.
Effect of method of thinning on wood production in a red pine plantation. Northern Journal of Applied Forestry. 20: 39-42.

Stiell, W.M.; Berry, A.B. 1973.
Yield of unthinned red pine plantations at the Petawawa Forest Experiment Station. Publ. 1320. Ontario, Canada: Canadian Forestry Service. 16 p.

Thrower, J.S. 1986.
Estimating site quality from early height growth in white spruce and red pine plantations in the Thunder Bay area. Thunder Bay, Ontario: Lakehead University. 143 p. M.Sc. thesis.

Van Eck, W.A.; Whiteside, E.P. 1958.
In: 1st North American forest soils conference proceedings. East Lansing, MI: Michigan State University: 218-226.

Walters, D.W.; Ek, A.R. 1993. Whole stand yield and density equations for fourteen forest types in Minnesota. Northern Journal of Applied Forestry. 10: 75-85.

Walter, R.; Epperson, B.K. 2001. Geographic pattern of genetic variation in *Pinus resinosa*: area of greatest diversity is not the origin of postglacial populations. Molecular Ecology. 10: 103-111.

Wilde, S.A.; Iyer, J.G.; Tanser, C.; et al. 1965.
Growth of Wisconsin coniferous plantations in relation to soils. Res. Bull. 262. Madison, WI: University Wisconsin-Madison. 81 p.

Wilson, L.F. 1987.
Saratoga spittlebug—its ecology and management. Agric. Handb. 657. Washington, DC: U.S. Department of Agriculture. 56 p.

Wilson, L.F.; Millers, I. 1983.
Pine root collar weevil—its ecology and management. Tech. Bull. 1675. Washington, DC: U. S. Department of Agriculture. 34 p.

Wilson, L.F.; Wilkinson, R.C.; Averill, R.C. 1992.
Redheaded pine sawfly—its ecology and management. Agric. Handb. 694. Washington, DC: U.S. Department of Agriculture. 54 p.

Woolsey, T.S., Jr.; Chapman, H.H. 1914.
Norway pine in the Lake States. Tech. Bull. 139. Washington, DC: U.S. Department of Agriculture. 42 p.

Wright, J.W.; Read, R.A.; Lester, D.T.; et al. 1972.
Geographic variation in red pine. Silvae Genetica. 21(6): 205-242.

Appendix: Useful Forestry Terminology

Terminology is an important tool for communication. The following terms are taken from Helms, J.A. (editor). 1998. The dictionary of forestry. The Society of American Foresters. Bethesda, MD. 210 p.

Age class: a distinct aggregation of trees originating from a single natural event or regeneration activity, or a grouping of trees

All-aged stand: a stand with trees of all or almost all age classes, including those of exploitable age.

Clearcut: a stand in which essentially all trees have been removed in one operation.

Cohort: a group of trees developing after a single disturbance, commonly consisting of trees of similar age, although it can include a considerable range of tree ages of seedling or sprout origin and trees that predate the disturbance.

Crop tree: any tree selected to become a component of a future commercial harvest.

Crown class: a category of tree based on its crown position relative to those of adjacent trees.

Crown cover, syn. **canopy cover:** the ground area covered by the crowns of trees or woody vegetation as delimited by the vertical projection of crown perimeters and commonly expressed as a percent of total ground area.

Crown density, syn. **canopy density:** the amount and compactness of foliage of the crowns of trees or shrubs.

Crown ratio (live crown ratio): the ratio of crown length to total tree height.

Even-aged stand: a stand of trees composed of a single age class in which the range of tree ages is usually ± 20 percent of rotation.

Extensive management: Management that balances timber and nontimber goals, generally with limited capital investments. In addition to timber production, management for wildlife habitat, water quality and quantity, recreation, biological diversity, and aesthetics are important.

Intermediate treatment: any treatment or tending designated to enhance growth, quality, vigor, and composition of the stand after establishment or regeneration and prior to harvest.

Multiaged (multicohort) stand: a stand with two or more age classes or cohorts.

Natural regeneration: the establishment of a plant or a plant age class from natural seeding, sprouting, suckering, or layering.

Overstory removal: the cutting of trees constituting an upper canopy layer to release trees or other vegetation in an understory.

Partial cutting: removal of only part of a stand for purposes other than regenerating a new age class; not considered a regeneration method.

Precommercial thinning (PCT): the removal of trees not for immediate financial return but to reduce stocking to concentrate growth on the more desirable trees.

Production management: often associated with high capital investments to ensure rapid dominance by desired species and includes treatments such as planting genetically improved stock, fertilization, competition control, thinning, and pruning.

Productivity: the capacity or ability of an environmental unit to produce organic material; the relative capacity of an area to sustain a supply of goods and services in the long run.

Regeneration: seedlings or saplings existing in a stand; the act of renewing tree cover by establishing young trees naturally or artificially.

Regeneration cut: any removal of trees intended to assist regeneration already present or to make regeneration possible.

Regeneration method: a cutting procedure by which a new age class is created; the major methods are clearcutting, seed tree, shelterwood, selection, and coppice. Regeneration methods are grouped in four categories: coppice, even-aged, two-aged, uneven-aged.

Release: a treatment designed to free young trees from undesirable, usually overtopping, competing vegetation. Treatments include cleaning, liberation, and weeding.

Reserve trees, syn. **green tree retention:** a tree, pole-size or larger, retained in either a dispersed or aggregated manner after the regeneration period under clearcutting, seed tree, shelterwood, group selection, or coppice methods.

Reserve management: conservation or restoration of forest land without considerations for financial returns or commodity goals. Can be either intrusive or nonintrusive in its impacts. When the goal is to conserve or protect a natural area from human-caused disturbances reserve management is nonintrusive. When the goal is to restore a condition or process, the management applications may be quite intrusive and intensive, e.g., prescribed fire, removal of exotic species.

Residual stand: a stand composed of trees remaining after any type of intermediate harvest.

Riparian zone: a terrestrial area, other than a coastal area, of variable width adjacent to and influenced by a perennial or intermittent body of water.

Rotation: in even-aged systems, the period between regeneration establishment and final cutting.

Seed tree: a tree left standing for the sole or primary purpose of providing seed; a method of natural regeneration.

Shelterwood: Stand is removed in a series of cuttings to promote the establishment of an even-aged stand.

Site: the area in which a plant or stand grows, considered in terms of its environment, particularly as this determined the type and quality of the vegetation the area can carry.

Site class: a classification of site quality, usually expressed in terms of ranges of dominant tree height at a given age or potential mean annual increment at culmination.

Site index: a species-specific measure of actual or potential forest productivity (site quality, usually for even-aged stands), expressed in terms of the average height of trees included in a specified stand component (defined as a certain number of dominants, codominants, or the largest and tallest trees per unit area) at a specified index or base age. The index is used as an indicator of site quality.

Site preparation: hand or mechanized manipulation of a site, designed to enhance the success of regeneration.

Site quality, syn. **site productivity:** the productive capacity of a site, usually expressed as volume production of a given species.

Stand improvement: an intermediate treatment made to improve the composition, structure, condition, health, and growth of even- or uneven-aged stands.

Stand structure: the horizontal and vertical distribution of components of a forest stand including the height, diameter, crown layers, and stems of trees, shrubs, herbaceous understory, snags, and down woody debris.

Stocking: an indication of growing-space occupancy relative to a preestablished standard. Common indices of stocking are based on percent occupancy, basal area, relative density, and crown competition factor.

Sustainability: the capacity of forests, ranging from stands to ecoregions, to maintain their health, productivity, diversity, and overall integrity, in the long run, in the context of human activity and use.

Thinning: a cultural treatment made to reduce stand density of trees primarily to improve growth, enhance forest health, or recover potential mortality.

Thinning interval, syn. thinning cycle: the period of time between successive thinning entries, usually in connection with even-aged stands.

Two-aged stand: a growing area with trees of two distinct age classes separated in age by more than ± 20 percent of rotation.

Two-aged system: a planned sequence of treatments designed to maintain and regenerate a stand with two age classes.

Underplanting: the setting out of young trees, or sowing of tree seed under an existing stand.

Uneven-aged stand: a stand with trees of three or more distinct age classes, either intimately mixed or in small groups.

Uneven-aged system: a planned sequence of treatments designed to maintain and regenerate a stand with three or more age classes.

Yield: the amount of wood that may be harvested from a particular type of forest stand by species, site, stocking, and management regime at various ages.

Appendix A.—Site Index Curves for Red Pine From Different Regions of North America

Carmean *et al.* (1989) provided seven sets of site index curves for red pine using various index ages. Although an index age of 50 is commonly used, some incorporate younger index ages. These curves are representative of height growth patterns for red pine based on total tree age, plantation age, and age measured at breast height (measured at 4.5 ft or 1.3 m above the ground) for specific regions across North America. In figures A1 and A2, we provide a graphical comparison of these published site index curves from distinctly different regions, grouping the curves according to a total or breast height index age. Equations to reproduce these curves are presented in the table A1.

The curves using a total age index age for Minnesota, Wisconsin, and Ontario are based on site indices of 50, 60, and 70 at an index age of 50. Site indices from Vermont are based on site indices of 40, 50, and 60 at an index age of 30 (fig. A1). Curves from Vermont indicate a more rapid early height. The Minnesota and Ontario curves have a similar form. The curves from Wisconsin suggest lower productivity, in terms of height growth, relative to other regions for red pine. The site index curves based on a breast height index age for Ontario are based on site indices of 50, 60, and 70 at an index age of 50 years at breast height. Site indices from Illinois are based on site indices of 30, 40, and 50 at 25 years at breast height. Site indices from New York are based on site indices of 20, 30, and 40 at an index age of 20 years at breast height (fig. A2). Curves from Vermont indicate a more rapid early height. The curves from Ontario indicate greater early height growth and greater productivity, in terms of height growth, than those from New York and Illinois. The curves from Illinois suggest productivity similar to the Ontario sites at younger ages but low productivity at older ages. The curves from New York indicate less productivity than those from Ontario but greater productivity than those from Illinois at older ages.

Table A1.—Parameter estimates for the equations used to create figures A1 and A2 (see Carmean *et al.* (1989) for details on the derivation of the parameters)

Region	b_1	b_2	b_3	b_4	b_5	Reference
Total age						
Minnesota Natural stands	1.8900	1.0000	-0.0198	1.3892	0.0000	Gevorkiantz 1957
Vermont Plantations (index age of 30 yrs)	2.0401	1.0003	-0.0361	1.7914	-0.0090	Hannah 1971
Wisconsin Plantations	2.6359	0.8259	-0.0389	21.5578	-0.6271	Wilde et al. 1965
Eastern Ontario Plantations	2.0434	0.9978	-0.0147	1.0937	-0.0035	Stiell and Berry 1973
Breast height age						
New York Natural stands (index age = 20 yrs bh)	19.0635	0.5885	-0.0111	3.3922	-0.3418	Richards et al. (1962)
Illinois Plantations (index age = 25 yrs bh)	0.7666	1.0909	-0.0733	3.2335	-0.2947	Gilmore (1968)
Central Ontario Natural stands	13.6713	0.5404	-0.0283	8.7720	-0.5308	Thrower (1986)

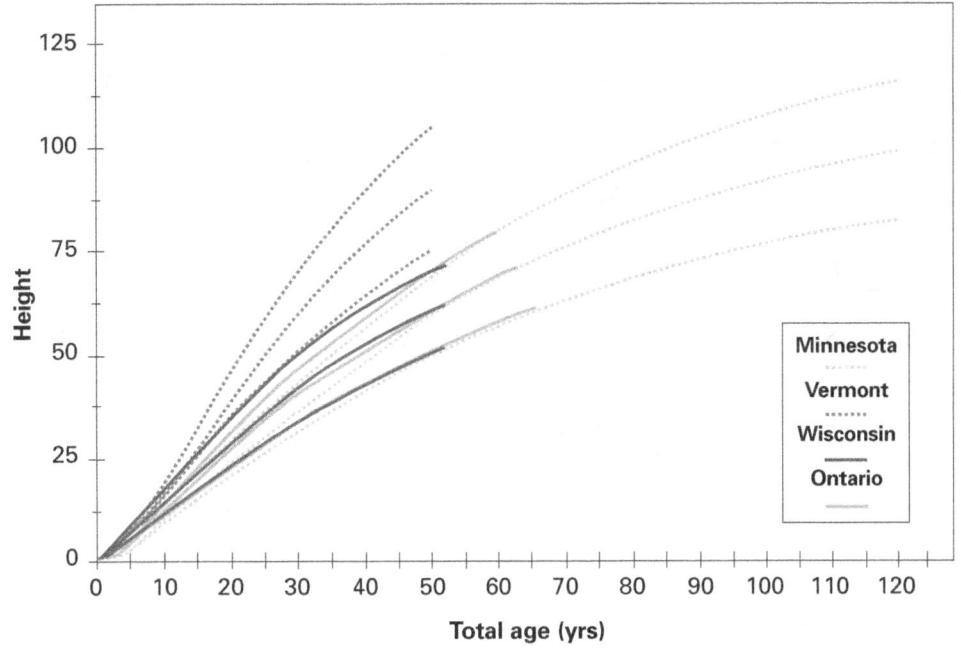

Figure A1.—
Comparison of site index curves based on total age from Minnesota, Vermont, Wisconsin, and Ontario. Site indices of 50, 60, and 70 are presented for each group of curves. Equation form: $H = b_1 S^{b2}[1 - \exp(b_3 A)]^{b4(S^{\wedge}b5)}$, where H = total height in feet, S = site index, A = total age, and b_i designates parameter estimates provided in table A1.

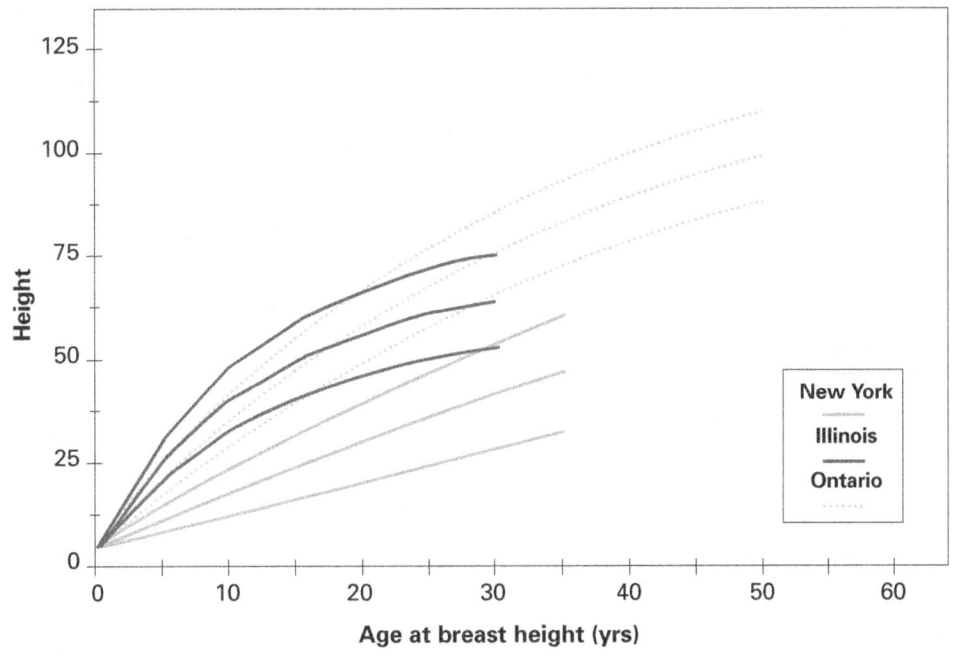

Figure A2.—
Comparison of site index curves based on breast height age from New York, Illinois, and Ontario. Site indices of 40, 50, and 60 are presented for each group of curves. Equation form: $H = 4.5 + b_1 S^{b2}[1 - \exp(b_3 Abh)]^{b4(S^{\wedge}b5)}$, where H = total height in feet, S = site index, Abh = breast height age measured at 4.5 ft, and b_i designates parameter estimates provided in table A1.

Appendix B.—Growth and Yield Equations and Tables for Red Pine Basal Area, Cubic Foot, Cord, and Board-foot Volume Growth

Table B1.—Tabulation of volume and d.b.h. prediction equations for red pine

Stand volume prediction equations

$V = 0.4085$ BAH, where V = total volume (ft^3 ac^{-1}), BA = basal area (in.), H = tree height (ft)
(Buckman 1962)

$V = 1.1606$ BA$^{1.0762}$H$^{0.6228}$, where V = total volume (ft^3 ac^{-1}), BA = basal area (in.), H = tree height (ft)
(Walters and Ek 1993)

$V_m = V \exp(-0.9979(t/D)^{3.0445} + -2.2294N^{-0.2621}(d/D)^{6.7081})$, where V_m = merchantable volume (ft^3 ac^{-1}), V = total volume (ft^3 ac^{-1}), D = quadratic mean d.b.h. (in.), N = number of trees per acre, t = minimum merchantable top diameter inside bark (in.), d = minimum merchantable d.b.h. (in.) (Mack and Burk 2004)

Individual tree volume prediction equations

$V = 0.002979$ D$^{1.7143}$H$^{1.1287}$, where
V = total volume (ft^3), D = d.b.h. (in.), and H = total tree height (ft)
(Fowler 1997)

$V = 0.0046$ D$^{1.8598}$H$^{0.9299}$, where
V = total volume (ft^3), D = d.b.h. (in.), and H = total tree height (ft)
(Gilmore *et al.* 2005)

$V = 0.1202$ D$^{2.0565}$, where
V = total volume (ft^3), and D = d.b.h. (in.)
(Gilmore *et al.* 2005)

Individual tree d.b.h. prediction from stump diameter

$D = 0.3462 + 0.7963D_{stmp}$, where D = d.b.h. (in.), D_{stmp} = stump diameter (in.) measured at 6 in. above ground
(Gilmore *et al.* 2005)

Individual tree volume prediction from stump diameter

$V = -8.417 + 1.8201 D_{stmp}$, where V = volume (ft^3), D_{stmp} = stump diameter (in.) measured at 6 in. above ground
(Gilmore *et al.* 2005)

Table B2.—Current annual basal area growth per acre for even-aged red pine stands by site, age, and stand density

Total age	Total height	Stand density – basal area per acre					
		30	60	90	120	150	180
Years	Feet	------------------------- Square feet per acre -------------------------					
SITE INDEX 75							
20	30	6.2	6.9	7.4	7.6	7.6	7.2
40	61	4.9	5.7	6.2	6.4	6.3	5.9
60	86	3.8	4.6	5.1	5.3	5.2	4.8
80	103	2.9	3.7	4.2	4.4	4.3	3.9
100	115	2.2	3.0	3.5	3.7	3.6	3.2
120	124	1.6	2.4	2.9	3.1	3.0	2.7
140	130	1.3	2.1	2.6	2.8	2.7	2.3
160	134	1.1	1.9	2.4	2.6	2.5	2.1
SITE INDEX 65							
20	26	5.5	6.3	6.8	7.0	6.9	6.5
40	53	4.2	5.0	5.5	5.7	5.6	5.3
60	74	3.2	4.0	4.4	4.6	4.6	4.2
80	89	2.3	3.1	3.5	3.8	3.7	3.3
100	100	1.5	2.3	2.8	3.0	2.9	2.6
120	107	1.0	1.8	2.3	2.5	2.4	2.0
140	112	.6	1.4	1.9	2.1	2.0	1.7
160	116	.5	1.3	1.8	2.0	1.9	1.5
SITE INDEX 55							
20	22	4.9	5.7	6.2	6.4	6.3	5.9
40	45	3.6	4.4	4.9	5.1	5.0	4.6
60	63	2.5	3.3	3.8	4.0	3.9	3.5
80	76	1.6	2.4	2.9	3.1	3.0	2.6
100	85	.9	1.7	2.2	2.4	2.3	1.9
120	91	.4	1.1	1.6	1.9	1.8	1.4
140	95	--	.8	1.3	1.5	1.4	1.0
160	98	--	.6	1.1	1.3	1.2	.8
SITE INDEX 45							
20	18	4.2	5.0	5.5	5.7	5.6	5.2
40	37	3.0	3.7	4.2	4.5	4.4	4.0
60	51	1.9	2.7	3.2	3.4	3.3	2.9
80	62	1.0	1.8	2.3	2.5	2.4	2.0
100	69	.2	1.0	1.5	1.7	1.6	1.3
120	74	--	.5	1.0	1.2	1.1	.7
140	78	--	.1	.6	.8	.8	.4
160	80	--	--	.5	.7	.6	.2

[1]BA growth = 1.6889 + .041066 (BA) - .00016303 (BA)^2 - .076958 (age) + .00022741 (age)^2 + .06441 (site index) (Buckman 1962).

Table B3.—Volume in cunits (100 cubic feet) per acre for even-aged red pine stands by site, age, and stand density

Total age	Total height	Stand density – basal area per acre					
		30	60	90	120	150	180
Years	Feet	------------Cunits per acre------------					
SITE INDEX 75							
20	30	3.7	7.3	11.0	14.7	18.4	22.0
40	61	7.5	14.9	22.4	29.9	37.3	44.8
60	86	10.5	21.0	31.6	42.1	52.6	63.2
80	103	12.6	25.2	37.8	50.4	63.0	75.6
100	115	14.1	28.2	42.2	56.3	70.4	84.5
120	124	15.2	30.4	45.4	60.7	75.9	91.1
140	130	15.9	31.8	47.7	63.6	79.6	95.5
160	134	16.4	32.8	49.2	65.6	82.0	98.4
SITE INDEX 65							
20	26	3.2	6.4	9.5	12.7	15.9	19.1
40	53	6.5	13.0	19.5	25.9	32.4	38.9
60	74	9.0	18.1	27.2	36.2	45.3	54.3
80	89	10.9	21.8	32.7	43.6	54.5	65.4
100	100	12.2	24.5	36.7	49.0	61.2	73.4
120	107	13.1	26.2	39.3	52.4	65.5	78.6
140	112	13.7	27.4	41.1	54.8	68.5	82.2
160	116	14.2	28.4	42.6	56.8	71.0	85.2
SITE INDEX 55							
20	22	2.7	5.4	8.1	10.8	13.5	16.2
40	45	5.5	11.0	16.5	22.0	27.5	33.0
60	63	7.7	15.4	23.1	30.8	38.6	46.3
80	76	9.3	18.6	27.9	37.2	46.5	55.8
100	85	10.4	20.8	31.2	41.6	52.0	62.4
120	91	11.1	22.3	33.4	44.6	55.7	66.8
140	95	11.6	23.2	34.9	46.5	58.1	69.8
160	98	12.0	24.0	36.0	48.0	60.0	72.0
SITE INDEX 45							
20	18	2.2	4.4	6.6	8.8	11.0	13.2
40	37	4.5	9.1	13.6	18.1	22.6	27.2
60	51	6.2	12.5	18.7	25.0	31.2	37.4
80	62	7.6	15.2	22.8	30.4	37.9	45.5
100	69	8.4	16.9	25.3	33.8	42.2	50.7
120	74	9.1	18.1	27.2	36.2	45.3	54.3
140	78	9.5	19.1	28.6	38.2	47.7	57.3
160	80	9.8	19.6	29.4	39.2	49.0	58.8

[1]Cubic feet = 0.4085 (basal area x height) (Buckman 1962).

[2]Total main stem volume in cunits from 6-inch stump to tip of tree. Estimated cunits to a 4-inch top d.i.b. can be obtained by subtracting 1.067 (basal area per acre in sq. ft. / ave. tree diameter in inches squared).

Table B4.—Current annual cubic foot growth per acre for even-aged red pine stands by site, age, and stand density

Total age	Total height	Stand density – basal area per acre					
		30	60	90	120	150	180
Years	Feet	--------------Cubic feet per acre--------------					
SITE INDEX 75							
20	30	101	131	158	182	203	218
40	61	142	180	210	232	246	253
60	86	147	188	218	237	246	244
80	103	131	174	204	221	225	217
100	115	110	154	184	199	200	188
120	124	85	129	158	172	171	159
140	130	72	117	146	159	156	137
160	134	63	109	139	152	149	130
SITE INDEX 65							
20	26	80	108	132	152	169	183
40	53	108	140	166	185	198	206
60	74	109	144	168	185	196	195
80	89	92	128	150	168	172	165
100	100	66	104	130	143	143	136
120	107	48	86	112	124	124	110
140	112	30	69	94	106	104	93
160	116	25	64	89	100	96	78
SITE INDEX 55							
20	22	61	83	103	119	133	144
40	45	80	107	129	145	155	160
60	63	75	106	128	143	151	150
80	76	56	87	109	121	124	118
100	85	36	69	91	103	105	96
120	91	19	48	71	86	86	74
140	95	--	36	58	68	67	54
160	98	--	26	48	57	54	39
SITE INDEX 45							
20	18	45	63	79	93	105	114
40	37	56	77	94	109	117	121
60	51	47	72	90	101	106	105
80	62	30	56	73	83	86	80
100	69	9	36	53	63	64	59
120	74	--	20	38	46	46	36
140	78	--	6	23	30	32	20
160	80	--	--	20	28	26	14

[1]Cubic feet growth = 0.4085 (basal area growth x height + height growth x basal area + basal area growth x height growth) (Buckman 1962).

Table B5.—Volume in cords per acre for even-aged red pine stands by site, age, and stand density

Total age	Total height	Stand density – basal area per acre					
		30	60	90	120	150	180
Years	Feet	--------------Cords per acre---------------					
SITE INDEX 75							
40	61	7.2	14.5	21.7	29.0	36.2	43.5
60	86	10.2	20.4	30.6	40.8	51.0	61.3
80	103	12.2	24.5	36.7	48.9	61.2	73.4
100	115	13.6	27.3	41.0	54.6	68.3	81.9
120	124	14.7	29.4	44.2	58.9	73.6	88.3
140	130	15.4	30.9	46.3	61.7	77.2	92.6
160	134	15.9	31.8	47.7	63.6	79.6	95.5
SITE INDEX 65							
40	53	6.3	12.6	18.9	25.2	31.5	37.8
60	74	8.8	17.6	26.4	35.1	43.9	52.7
80	89	10.6	21.1	31.7	42.3	52.8	63.4
100	100	11.9	23.7	35.6	47.5	59.4	71.2
120	107	12.7	25.4	38.1	50.8	63.5	76.2
140	112	13.3	26.6	39.9	53.2	66.5	79.8
160	116	13.8	27.5	41.3	55.1	68.9	82.6
SITE INDEX 55							
40	45	5.3	10.7	16.0	21.4	26.7	32.0
60	63	7.5	15.0	22.4	29.9	37.4	44.9
80	76	9.0	18.0	27.1	36.1	45.1	54.1
100	85	10.1	20.2	30.3	40.4	50.5	60.5
120	91	10.8	21.6	32.4	43.2	54.0	64.8
140	95	11.3	22.6	33.8	45.1	56.4	67.7
160	98	11.6	23.3	34.9	46.5	58.2	69.8
SITE INDEX 45							
40	37	4.4	8.8	13.2	17.6	22.0	26.4
60	51	6.1	12.1	18.2	24.2	30.3	36.3
80	62	7.4	14.7	22.1	29.4	36.8	44.2
100	69	8.2	16.4	24.6	32.8	41.0	49.2
120	74	8.8	17.6	26.4	35.1	43.9	52.7
140	78	9.3	18.5	27.8	37.0	46.3	55.6
160	80	9.5	19.0	28.5	38.0	47.5	57.0

[1]Cords = 0.003958 (basal area x height). Rough cords for trees 3.6 inches d.b.h. and larger to a 3-inch top d.i.b. (Buckman 1962).
[2]Must be in trees 3.6 inches d.b.h. and larger.

Table B6.—Current annual cordwood growth per acre for even-aged red pine stands by site, age, and stand density

Total age	Total height	Stand density – basal area per acre					
		30	60	90	120	150	180
Years	Feet	-------------Cords per acre---------------					
SITE INDEX 75							
40	61	1.3	1.7	2.0	2.2	2.4	2.4
60	86	1.4	1.8	2.1	2.3	2.4	2.4
80	103	1.3	1.7	2.0	2.1	2.2	2.1
100	115	1.1	1.5	1.8	1.9	1.9	1.8
120	124	.8	1.2	1.5	1.7	1.6	1.5
140	130	.7	1.1	1.4	1.5	1.5	1.3
160	134	.6	1.0	1.3	1.5	1.4	1.3
SITE INDEX 65							
40	53	1.0	1.4	1.6	1.8	1.9	2.0
60	74	1.1	1.4	1.6	1.8	1.9	1.9
80	89	.9	1.2	1.5	1.6	1.7	1.6
100	100	.6	1.0	1.3	1.4	1.4	1.3
120	107	.5	.8	1.1	1.2	1.2	1.1
140	112	.3	.7	.9	1.0	1.0	.9
160	116	.2	.6	.9	1.0	.9	.8
SITE INDEX 55							
40	45	.8	1.0	1.2	1.4	1.5	1.5
60	63	.7	1.0	1.2	1.4	1.5	1.5
80	76	.5	.8	1.1	1.2	1.2	1.1
100	85	.4	.7	.9	1.0	1.0	.9
120	91	.2	.5	.7	.8	.8	.7
140	95	--	.3	.6	.7	.6	.5
160	98	--	.3	.5	.6	.5	.4
SITE INDEX 45							
40	37	.5	.7	.9	1.0	1.1	1.2
60	51	.5	.7	.9	1.0	1.0	1.0
80	62	.3	.5	.7	.8	.8	.8
100	69	.1	.3	.5	.6	.6	.6
120	74	--	.2	.4	.4	.4	.3
140	78	--	.1	.2	.3	.3	.2
160	80	--	--	.2	.3	.2	.1

[1]Cordwood growth = .003958 (basal area growth x height + height growth x basal area + basal area growth x height growth) (Buckman 1962).

[2]Must be in trees 3.6 inches d.b.h. and larger.

Table B7.—Volume in M board feet per acre for even-aged red pine stands by site, age, and stand density

Total age	Total height	Stand density – basal area per acre					
		30	60	90	120	150	180
Years	Feet	--------------M board feet per acre--------------					
SITE INDEX 75							
60	86	5.4	10.8	16.1	21.5	26.9	32.3
80	103	6.4	12.9	19.3	25.8	32.2	38.6
100	115	7.2	14.4	21.6	28.8	35.9	43.1
120	124	7.8	15.5	23.3	31.0	38.8	46.5
140	130	8.1	16.3	24.4	32.5	40.6	48.8
160	134	8.4	16.8	25.1	33.5	41.9	50.3
SITE INDEX 65							
60	74	4.6	9.2	13.9	18.5	23.1	27.8
80	89	5.6	11.1	16.7	22.3	27.8	33.4
100	100	6.3	12.5	18.8	25.0	31.3	37.5
120	107	6.7	13.4	20.1	26.8	33.4	40.1
140	112	7.0	14.0	21.0	28.0	35.0	42.0
160	116	7.2	14.5	21.8	29.0	36.3	43.5
SITE INDEX 55							
60	63	3.9	7.9	11.8	15.8	19.7	23.6
80	76	4.7	9.5	14.2	19.0	23.8	28.5
100	85	5.3	10.6	15.9	21.3	26.6	31.9
120	91	5.7	11.4	17.1	22.8	28.4	34.1
140	95	5.9	11.9	17.8	23.8	29.7	35.6
160	98	6.1	12.2	18.4	24.5	30.6	36.8
SITE INDEX 45							
60	51	3.2	6.4	9.6	12.8	15.9	19.1
80	62	3.9	7.8	11.6	15.5	19.4	23.3
100	69	4.4	8.6	12.9	17.3	21.6	25.9
120	74	4.6	9.2	13.9	18.5	23.1	27.8
140	78	4.9	9.8	14.6	19.5	24.4	29.3
160	80	5.0	10.0	15.0	20.0	25.0	30.0

[1]Board feet = 2.084 (basal area x height). Board-foot volume by Scribner Dec. C. log rule for trees 7.6 inches d.b.h. to a 6-inch top d.i.b. (Buckman 1962).
[2]Must be in trees 7.6 inches d.b.h. and larger.

Table B8.—Current annual board-foot growth per acre for even-aged red pine stands by site, age, and stand density

		Stand density – basal area per acre					
Total age	Total height	30	60	90	120	150	180
Years	Feet	--------------Board feet per acre--------------					
SITE INDEX 75							
60	86	751	959	1112	1211	1255	1245
80	103	670	887	1039	1126	1148	1105
100	115	560	785	936	1016	1023	958
120	124	433	659	807	878	871	812
140	130	365	595	743	810	795	699
160	134	320	556	709	777	762	662
SITE INDEX 65							
60	74	556	737	856	943	999	993
80	89	467	654	766	860	878	841
100	100	339	531	661	728	732	694
120	107	242	440	571	634	630	560
140	112	153	352	482	541	530	472
160	116	127	327	454	509	491	400
SITE INDEX 55							
60	63	382	539	655	732	769	765
80	76	286	445	556	619	635	602
100	85	185	352	466	527	534	488
120	91	95	247	361	436	436	379
140	95	--	184	295	348	340	273
160	98	--	135	244	291	276	201
SITE INDEX 45							
60	51	242	365	457	516	542	537
80	62	155	284	374	425	437	410
100	69	48	182	273	320	325	300
120	74	--	102	192	236	233	183
140	78	--	29	116	155	161	103
160	80	--	--	102	142	131	71

[1]Board-foot growth = 2.084 (basal area growth x height + height growth x basal area + basal area growth x height growth) (Buckman 1962).
[2]Must be in trees 7.6 inches d.b.h. and larger.

Appendix C.—Rotation Ages Calculated at Various Site Indices and Densities for Red Pine

Table C1.—Rotation ages for maximum mean annual board-foot growth in red pine periodically thinned to a given stand density, by site index

Planted trees/acre	Basal area density after periodic thinning											
	30	60	90	120	150	180	30	60	90	120	150	180
SITE INDEX 75												
	Rotation age – years						Board feet per acre per year					
400	63	93	103	113	118	103	331	614	831	980	1013	841
800	83	103	103	113	143	123	302	561	775	894	867	654
SITE INDEX 65												
	Rotation age – years						Board feet per acre per year					
400	93	83	103	103	123	98	247	471	654	774	732	618
800	83	103	103	133	148	118	237	447	605	676	583	415
SITE INDEX 55												
	Rotation age – years						Board feet per acre per year					
400	93	93	103	118	113	78	189	367	496	555	492	394
800	93	103	123	143	138	143	184	336	451	448	340	161
SITE INDEX 45												
	Rotation age – years						Board feet per acre per year					
400	98	108	123	118	88	88	124	245	336	329	263	263
800	103	123	128	138	--	--	113	217	259	226	--	--

Source: Unpublished red pine yield tables for managed plantations and natural stands in the Lake States. Computer program developed by Lundgren (1971) from growth and yield studies at the Northern Conifers Laboratory.

[1]International 1/4 inch board-foot volumes in trees 9 inches d.b.h. and larger to a 6- inch top d.i.b.

[2]Mean annual growth did not culminate prior to 153 years of age in these high-density stands.

Gilmore, Daniel W.; Palik, Brian J.

    2006. **A revised managers handbook for red pine in the North Central Region.** Gen. Tech. Rep. NC-264. St. Paul, MN: U.S. Department of Agriculture, Forest Service, North Central Research Station. 55 p.

    This new version of the Red Pine Managers Guide gathers up-to-date information from many disciplines to address a wide range of red pine management issues. It provides guidance on managing red pine on extended rotations with a focus on landscape-scale objectives along with the traditional forest management tools focusing on production silviculture. The insect and disease portion of this guide has been expanded to include the latest information on forest protection.

KEY WORDS: Forest health, forest protection, growth and yield, landscape management, silviculture.